THE RUDIMENTS OF

PRACTICAL BRICKLAYING

IN SIX SECTIONS:

GENERAL PRINCIPLES OF BRICKLAYING; ARCH DRAWING,
CUTTING, AND SETTING; DIFFERENT KINDS OF
POINTING; PAVING, TILING, MATERIALS; SLATING, AND
PLASTERING; PRACTICAL GEOMETRY,
MENSURATION, ᴇᴛᴄ.

By ADAM HAMMOND

ILLUSTRATED WITH SIXTY-EIGHT WOODCUTS

FIFTH EDITION, CAREFULLY REVISED, WITH ADDITIONS

LONDON
CROSBY LOCKWOOD AND CO.
7, STATIONERS' HALL COURT, LUDGATE HILL
1885

[2008]

PREFACE.

THE object of this little work is to assist young beginners and others who, though in the trade many years, have not had the opportunity of seeing so much of the higher branches of practice as they might desire. I also trust it will not be thought unworthy the notice of the more skilful mechanic.

The language I have used is as simple as the subject would allow, and the terms used are those well understood in the trade; for it is to be regretted that the greater number of books upon "building construction" are written in such terms that it is very difficult for the majority of working men to understand their meaning without continually referring to a technical dictionary.

In speaking of foundations, I have said nothing of those which are formed in soft situations, upon piles, or woodwork of any description; for in such cases the bricklayer has nothing to do with the work until the foundation is made.

I have no hesitation in saying the methods here employed in drawing and cutting arches, also in mixing the materials and executing the different sorts of pointing, are practically the best, and those generally adopted by the most experienced workmen.

For the sake of those who have not had an opportunity of learning Geometry and Mensuration, such problems are given as are generally required in bricklaying.

The tables, and also the quantities of materials, have been carefully calculated; and during the eighteen years I have been in practice I have proved them correct.

ADAM HAMMOND.

NOTE TO FIFTH EDITION.

THE author views with satisfaction the extensive sale of this little work, and also the favour with which it is generally received, having already run through four editions since its publication.

The present edition has undergone a thorough revision, and various additions and corrections, thought necessary for the improvement and utility of the work, have been made throughout.

A. H.

LONDON, *August*, 1884.

CONTENTS.

SECTION I.

GENERAL PRINCIPLES OF BRICKLAYING.

SECTION V.

SLATER AND PLASTERER'S WORK.

SECTION VI.

PRACTICAL GEOMETRY AND MENSURATION.

A FEW REMARKS ON MENSURATION OF
BRICKLAYERS' WORK.

THE RUDIMENTS

OF

PRACTICAL BRICKLAYING.

———•———

SECTION I.

GENERAL PRINCIPLES OF BRICKLAYING.

THE Business of a Bricklayer not only consists in the execution of all kinds of brickwork, but it also includes rough stonework or "walling," paving, and tiling, both plain and ornamental; and (in many parts of the country) slating and plastering is united with the above-named business. The bricklayer also superintends all excavations and concreting for ordinary building purposes.

In preparing for the erection of most buildings the first things required are the plans, elevations, sections, &c., and upon these too much care cannot be bestowed so that the foreman may get them thoroughly impressed upon his mind, for by so doing very many mistakes will be prevented.

FOUNDATIONS.

The ground should be set out from a given line, such as the face-line of the building, and wood stakes driven into the ground on which to

B

strain the different lines. Great care is required in squaring out the foundation trenches so that the brickwork (when built) shall stand in the centre of them, and not all on one side of the trench and none on the other, which is but too frequently the case, for the greatest care is usually taken when the *wall line* is drawn.

The sides of the trenches ought to be upright, so that there is not a less area for the concrete at the bottom than at the top: for upon this depends the strength of the superstructure.

Should the ground be "*an incline plane*," or *unlevel*, it is much better to bench the ground carefully out—that is, cut out the bottom of the trench in horizontal steps.* The concrete will then be of a more uniform thickness, and the settlement of the building will be more regular, as nearly all buildings are built with materials that will settle little or much, and it does not so much matter *as long as the settlement is perfectly regular*, but the evil effects are seen when it is greater in one part than in another, and, in concrete as well as brickwork, the greater the thickness the more will be the settlement.

It is usual to drive stakes in the *bottom* of the trenches to show the level of concrete; but perhaps it would be better, if possible, to drive these stakes in the *sides* of the trenches, leaving just enough projecting out to level them with, for very often by shooting the concrete into the

* Taking care that each step shall be 3, 6, 9, or 12 inches above the next lower one if the work above is to be built 4 courses to the foot.

trench the stakes are knocked further into the ground and the concrete levelled to them, thereby causing a great deal of trouble when the brick-work is begun.

CONCRETE.

The "limes" generally used for concreting in this country are obtained from Dorking in Surrey, and Rochester in Kent,* besides other places where the grey limestone is to be obtained.

This lime is ground and mixed with ballast while in a powdered state; it is then wetted and turned over twice, to mix them well together; this is then wheeled in barrows to an elevated position and thrown into the trenches, and after-wards levelled to receive the brickwork. This kind of concrete is mixed in the proportions of one part of lime to six or seven parts of gravel. Although this kind of concrete is very much used in and about London, it is considered a very imperfect method, although economical as regards the labour: it proves most expensive in the material, for if the work was properly executed it would not require nearly so much of the latter.

The method of concreting which is thought by most engineers to be the best is, to reduce the lime to the state of a thick paste, and then it is made into a soft mortar by mixing about an equal quantity of sand with it before it is mixed with the gravel; and instead of shooting it down from a height and leaving it to settle by itself, it

* This is open to *local* circumstances.

ought to be wheeled in upon a level and beaten with a rammer; for it is thought by being thrown from a height the materials separate, and by so doing some parts get more lime than they ought to have, while others get but very little.

Of course this kind of artificial foundations is not required where there is a natural one, such as a bed of rock, hard gravel, or anything that is thought sound enough to sustain the weight of the building.

DRAINS.

As soon as the concreting is completed, all levels should be taken for the drains, &c., so that the brickwork is not cut about afterwards; and if the pipes are very large it would be better to leave out the brickwork so that they may be fixed after the work has had time to settle. And if a small arch of brick is turned over each of these pipes, it will be found very convenient should they want repairing or cleaning at any time.

FOOTINGS.

In all buildings of any importance it is usual to build a certain number of courses as *footings*

Fig. 1.

(as shown in Fig. 1) to give the walls a greater bearing; and where the building is principally constructed with piers, such as a great many warehouses, &c., inverted arches are turned for the purpose of distributing the weight over the

whole length of the foundation, as shown in
Fig. 2. Sometimes these are formed in the

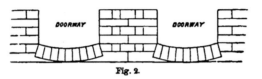

Fig. 2.

footing courses, but generally upon the top of the
footings.

BONDING.

The next thing of importance is the bonding
of the brickwork, of which a great deal may be
said, for this is a very important part of bricklaying.

Old English is that which is used in nearly all
buildings where strength is the principal object,
as it is the strongest of any, on account of the
greater quantity of " headers " used, and also
because there are less broken bricks required to
fill in with.

But the appearance is not considered so neat as
Flemish bond.

Figs. 3 and 4 show two successive courses of
Old English bond : in all cases the inside headers
and stretchers should be opposite those of the
same names on the outside (*i.e.* A is opposite B,
Fig. 3). If this rule is strictly adhered to, there
will always be correct quarter bond throughout
the whole thickness of the wall.

Very often but little attention is paid   to

the *middle of the wall,* so long as the faces are

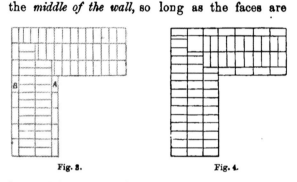

Fig. 3.   Fig. 4.

kept right, although it is of quite as much importance.

Figs. 5 and 6 show the bonding of the face and

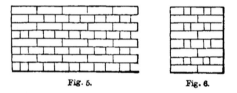

Fig. 5.   Fig. 6.

end of what is called an 18-inch, or two-brick wall, in Old English bond.

Flemish Bond (Fig. 7) is very much used for

house building, owing to its
neater appearance. But very
often the inside of the house
is Old English; and when the
walls are built in this manner,
the heading bricks of the Fle-
Fig. 7.

mish work are halved ("bats," as they are more
generally called) every second course; and by so

doing the inside of the wall gets a half-brick tie into the face work.

In Flemish bond the headers and stretchers are laid in turns in each course, as shown in Fig. 7.

In all cases where quoins are to be got up at different parts of the building, *gauge-rods* should be used after the work has been levelled, and a nail or something of the kind knocked into the work at the level of which it is intended to gauge from.

If this is not done, different bricklayers will raise their work some more and some less than the others, thereby causing the work to get out of level.

If it be possible every man ought to be kept on his own work ; then he is more likely to take an interest in that particular part. But if they are not, when one man goes on to another's work there is often a great deal of fault-finding, and if the work is wrong it is simply impossible to find out who it was that did it.

Architects are generally under the impression that the bricks used in and about London are something under 9 inches in length, $4\frac{1}{2}$ inches wide, and $2\frac{1}{2}$ inches thick ; the thickness may be about right, but the other dimensions are decidedly wrong. This causes a great deal of trouble to the bricklayer when working to plans ; because he is asked to build a wall (for instance) eighteen inches thick, the regular bond of a two-brick wall, which is impossible to do without cutting the bricks, as they are from *nine inches* to *nine inches and a quarter* in length, and never less than the former.

Again, as regards the width of the brick, if it were 4½ inches, it would be impossible to build, say, a 9-inch wall, giving it the proper wall-joint,[*] without sailing the stretching course over; which, of course, is against all rule.

This is the reason (the bricks being only 4¼ inches wide) that bricklayers have to cut so many three-quarters, or long bats, in face-work, to keep the cross-joints' quarter-bond on the stretchers.

Broken Bond.—A great deal of this might be done away with if the plans were got out to suit the bricks more than they usually are; for very often we see pairs between openings sixteen, twenty, and thirty inches in length, without the least regard to what the bricks will work; thereby causing a great quantity of brick to be wasted, more labour, and then the work is nothing near so strong as if the work had been arranged so that the bricks would work without cutting them.

It is very necessary, when laying the first course on the footings, that all doorways, windows, and other openings, should be measured, and the bond properly set out, so that there is no difficulty when the work is up, ready to receive them, and the perpends † are kept throughout the height of the building.

Herringbone Bonding, as shown in Fig. 7A, is

---

[*] Three-eighths of an inch between the bricks.
† The cross joints in a perpendicular line.

greatly used for cores of arches and other places
where something different to the regular plain
work is required in the shape of ornamentation.
But it has but very little tie with the inside work.
This work should be begun and continued with

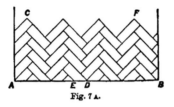

Fig. 7 A.

the set square of 45 degrees; and if the bricks
are all of one length, the joints will all cut
straight with one another, showing so many
oblique lines at an angle of 45 degrees with the
horizontal from where the herringbone started;
that is, place the set square upon the base-line
A B, Fig. 7 A, in such a manner that the right
angle of the square shall be uppermost and the
longest side upon the line, and as it is drawn
along from A to B, or from B to A (if the work
is right), it will cut in a line with the joints C D,
E F, &c., and as the work proceeds it will be
necessary to either hold up a levelled straight-
edge and work the square upon it, or otherwise
draw a line perfectly level, and so hold the
square to it.

But to do this kind of work properly, it is
really necessary that *every brick should be of one
length*, that is, what three courses of bricks will
measure upright when laid temporarily with joints

the same thickness as those required for the herringboning. If the joints are to be small very often the bricks will have to be cut short, and this gives it a better appearance than having thick joints, and, beside, it is much stronger work if it is well grouted in at the back. But in all cases let the grout be of the same kind as the work is built with.

Fig. 8 represents another style of herringbone. This is called " *Double Herringbone,*" on account of two bricks being worked instead of one, as shown in Fig. 7A. The working of this is much the same as Fig. 7A, but perhaps a little more difficult in

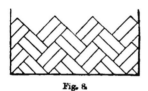

Fig. 8.

the arrangement of the bricks; nevertheless the joints must cut one with another just the same as the "perpends" of plain brickwork. If the bricks are cut to 8½ inches in length the work will show a neat joint, and there will be less trouble in keeping the work right. But it is very frequently done without any care being taken to get the bricks to suit the work, or to keep them in their proper places while laying them.

Garden Wall Bond, as it is generally called, is that which is in practice usually when building 9-inch walling, which requires to be faced on both sides; and as the headers cause an unsightly appearance if worked through too often, on account of their different lengths, it is usual to work three "stretchers" between two "headers," instead of one, as in Flemish bond.

DAMP COURSES.

As soon as the work is above ground it ought to receive a course of something to prevent the damp from rising up into the walls, and for this purpose *asphalte* is often used to cover the walls. But where this is difficult to be obtained a *double course of slates bedded in Portland cement* will generally answer the same purpose; but they must be so bonded, that no two joints shall be over each other to allow the dampness to rise between them.

AIR BRICKS.

Where the ground-floors of the building are to be laid with boards, air bricks should be built in the face of the walls, and a passage left through, so that the air can freely circulate under the floors, and by leaving two or three bricks out in different places of the inside or parting walls to any part of the building where required.

WOOD AND IRON BONDING.

In addition to the regular bonding of brickwork, as before described, a further security is sometimes provided in the form of *bond timber;* that is, long lengths of wood cut to the form of a 4½-inch course of bricks, and so laid throughout the length of the walls to answer as a longitudinal tie, and also to keep the pairs between openings steady until the work is thoroughly set.

But of late years this has been superseded to a great extent by *hoop-iron*, both on account of the wood shrinking when it gets dry and so causing the work to settle, also, in case of fire, to have material in the building as little inflammable as possible.

The hoop-iron is laid at different stages throughout the whole building. This is sometimes tarred and drawn through sand, to protect the iron from contact with the mortar; but it is more frequently laid between courses of bricks, and built with Portland cement, without being tarred.

JOINTS.

It is very necessary that all joints should be kept of one thickness; for if one piece of brickwork is raised with thick bricks and another with thin (as it often is when two sorts of bricks are used—one for outside and the other for inside) the work done with the thickest joints will *settle* more than the other, thereby causing the wall to overhang or batter: this is the case with mortar joints. Cement acts in the reverse manner, on account of its *swelling* properties; therefore in both cases it is considered very unsound work.

Portland cement having this *swelling property*, it is well adapted for underpinning old walls, where the ground has been taken out for cellars, &c., below the foundations; but slate ought not to be driven into the joint between the old and new work for the purpose of wedging it tight, for the cement will not take hold of the slate to any great extent; besides, if the joint is well filled up with cement, it will expand sufficiently to wedge itself perfectly tight.

WINDOW SILLS.

Where these are of stone, it is much better to leave the brickwork out at the reveals just large enough so that the sill can be fixed after the brickwork is up and settled; if not, the weight of the brickwork upon each end of it will very likely break the sill, owing to the greater settlement of the work between the windows (where there are the greater number of mortar joints) than there is directly underneath the sill.

Bricks ought to be well wetted in summer time, so as to exclude the air which fills up the pores; but be careful that they are not wet *if there is any likelihood of frost,* as it takes fast hold of work that is damp, not only causing the joints to burst out, but sometimes greatly disturbing the bricks.

All walls ought to be thoroughly "flushed" up every successive course with soft mortar or cement, as the case may be. This is sometimes preferred to "grout," because the latter, being so much thinner, will naturally shrink more when setting; so, if there is the proper wall-joint, there is little doubt but what the mortar-flushing makes the soundest work. There is a common but very evil practice in many places of *building walls with mortar and afterwards grouting them in with Portland cement mixed with sand.* Where this is the case, the weight of the building must be considered as standing upon the grout alone, for it is well known "*that cement swells and mortar shrinks;*" therefore, whenever the cement grout runs under the bricks, it will surely lift them off the mortar bed; and, instead of strengthening the work, it has a great tendency to weaken it. Great care should be taken, in building walls of any considerable length, that the line is kept perfectly straight from end to end; because if the line is drawn tight *one course and another loose*, there will be "brick and brick" in some places, and a thick joint in others, which gives the work a very bad appearance. In fact *the line* ought to be "*looked through*" every course.

Rubble Work.

In many parts of England rubble work is done to a great extent with flint and other stones; and in such cases it is usual to have brick quoins, and these are generally "ashlared," as shown in Fig. 9. In London this name is applied to stone-facing.

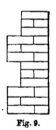

Fig. 9.

Although flint-stones are not so well adapted for works requiring great strength as bricks, still they answer very well for what they are generally used, that is, cottage and wall-building, &c., but it is not advisable to use *sea stones* for house-building, on account of the salt clinging to them causing the walls to turn damp in wet weather.

No flint-stones ought to be *used* in wet weather,

or if they are at all wet; for this is the cause of many a wall falling to the ground.

BRICK AND STONE COMBINED.

When the building is composed of brick and stone, which it very often is, the bricklayer and mason ought to be careful to get their work arranged to suit each other, as brickwork cannot be built to the specified thickness without a very great deal of extra labour and waste of material. For instance, a wall supposed to be built 2 feet 3 inches in thickness very often cannot be worked under 2 feet 3¾ inches because the bricks are full 9 inches long, and a wall never ought to be built without allowing room for the mortar to go between each brick in the middle of the wall.

And so by the stonemason cutting and working the stone that has to pass through the wall three-quarters of an inch longer, it would save the cutting of each course of bricks from beginning to end of the wall.

And if this is not thought of in the foundations, it will very likely cause a vast amount of trouble when the work is further advanced. Again, in arch work, &c., where drawing is required, and stone and brick are to be used, it is best for both mason and bricklayer to work to one drawing; for it is possible for two separate drawings to be different, so causing confusion when fixing the work; and it very often happens when anything is set out wrong through the oversight, carelessness, or ignorance of the foreman, the blame is directly thrown on to the workman for the purpose of clearing himself. But this is a cowardly way of doing business, and cannot be too much condemned.

LIMES, CEMENTS, ETC.

Of limes, *blue lias* is reckoned the best in this country, because it is equally adapted for work below water-level or for moist situations as for dry ones. But it is not generally used for ordinary building purposes, principally on account of its taking but a very small proportion of sand before its setting properties are weakened; so it is thought best only to use little more sand than lime in the mixing.

This lime must not be made into mortar a long time before it is required as other limes often are, or else it will get so hard that it will be of very little use for the purpose of laying bricks.

This lime will take less water than the other limes usually do; and it ought to be slacked several hours before it is made into mortar, as some parts will take much longer than others.

The principal supplies of lias limestone are obtained from Aberthaw, near Cardiff, in Wales; Barrow, near Mount Sorrel, in Leicestershire; and Watchet.

Dorking and Halling Limes. — These may be considered the principal limes used in and about London for making mortar, owing to their taking a greater quantity of sand than any other before their setting properties are weakened, the usual proportions being three or four parts of sand to one of lime.   But it must be remembered that very often it is not the *quantity* but the *quality* of sand that destroys the lime; for the cleaner and sharper the sand, the better the mortar will be.

These limes are obtained from Dorking in Surrey; and between Rochester and Maidstone in Kent.

Chalk Lime is seldom used in London for outside work, because it sets so slowly, and in damp places never sets at all.   But it is used to a great extent for plastering the inside of houses, &c., where there is no dampness; and, although it is not used in London for outside work, it is very much used in many parts of the country, where it is very cheap, and better limes are not so easily obtained.

Cements.——The cements used by the builder are of various kinds; such as *Portland* and *Roman* for external, and *Keen's* and *Martin's* for internal, decorations.

Portland Cement is considered the best for general use, owing to its fine setting properties and its cheapness; for it takes a greater quantity of sand than any other before it is much weakened.   This is made in different parts of the country, principally from the cement-stone found in the London clay at Harwich in Essex, and the Isle of Sheppey in Kent; and will take two or three parts of sand to one of cement for ordinary purposes.

But whenever it is required to set directly or for water-work, it is best to use it in its pure state. For although sand does not prevent its setting very hard after a few days, it stops its setting directly.

All sands used for making up lime and cement into mortar should be as free from clay or dirt as possible, and the sharper the better. If this is neglected, the best limes or cements are soon ruined.

Owing to the great demand for Portland cement, a great many manufacturers have been induced to bring out an artificial kind, and this is as much used as that made from the cement-stone. The greater part of this is made with clay obtained from the sides of the River Medway in Kent, mixed with a definite proportion of chalk from the pits in the same district, and so manufactured as to produce a cement nearly equal to the original.

Roman cement, although possessing many good qualities, is greatly inferior to Portland, and therefore is but little used by the builder.

Keen's and Martin's cements are in appearance a great deal like plaster of Paris, but they set much slower, thereby giving the workman more time to add finish to his work before it gets hard. They are almost always used for work which requires a hard and beautiful finish. But in no case should they be used for outside work, or in any place where they are exposed to the action of water, as they are like all pure limes, partly soluble in water.

WOOD BRICKS.

Wherever woodwork is to be fixed to the walls

(such as door and window frames, angle beads, skirting boards, &c.) wood bricks, or, rather, wood joints, should be used—that is, pieces of board the length and width of a brick, and about three-eighths of an inch thick, should be laid between two courses of bricks instead of the mortar joint. These will be found far better than having wood bricks the full size of the ordinary brick, because the latter generally shrink, and so become loose. When the inside is to be matched-lined instead of plastered, it is best to lay a joint of this sort throughout the length of the wall inside. If these are laid about three feet apart from floor to ceiling, there will be no plugging afterwards in fixing the matchboards.

FROST.

If the brickwork is carried on in frosty weather, all walls must be carefully covered up with weatherboards, straw, or something that will protect them; if not, the frost will penetrate into the work, and greatly destroy the strength of all that which is damp.

If Portland cement is mixed with mortar the frost does not take hold of it so much as it does if mortar alone.

TOOTHINGS.

When necessary to carry one part of the building up without the other, the walls where they join ought to be " racked " back, if possible ; if not, they ought to be toothed, as shown in Fig. 10, so as to avoid as much as possible upright toothings from bottom to top of the wall.

Thick and Thin Joints.

So much has been said by different writers about *thick* joints, that it is quite unnecessary for me to say that they are a very great evil, as they cause settlements. But perhaps a little ought to be said about very *thin* ones, for it is well known that the bricks made in most yards are not all of one thickness; and it is possible to buy a quantity of bricks all made in *one* yard, and to find two or

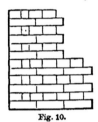

Fig. 10.

three different sizes—some as much as a quarter of an inch thicker than others. Therefore, when these thick bricks are laid, it is found impossible to keep down to the gauge to which the thin ones are laid with a joint of the same thickness.

The result is, the bricklayer does not spread out a bed to receive the brick, as he usually does, but he "butters" it—that is, he draws a little mortar, as fine as he can get, upon the front and back edges of the brick, and then lays it, leaving an air-passage under every one. This is almost as bad as thick joints, for it is evidently not bedded at all. This is very bad work, but the bricklayer cannot be blamed for it.

Profiles.

In building retaining walls, either upright or battering, or, in fact, any kind of work that is to be racked back to receive additional work, it is often

found convenient to erect profiles upright or battering, as the case may be, with the face of the wall,
and gauged according to the gauge of the work from
bottom to top—and so strain the line to it; by this
means the work is kept right both on the face and
bed.

These profiles answer very well for setting
arches when they are required in advance of the
other work; for they can be easily set up at each
end, and the line for the face of the arches drawn
to them, and afterwards drawn perfectly level
over the crown of the arches, to level up the
brickwork between them—and in *this* case it will
answer the purpose of both level and plumb-rule.

TRAMMELS.

Where work is to be cut to receive inverted
arches, such as the bottom half of a wheel arch,
and also cores to receive any other arches, it is
much best to fix trammels. These are fixed to
the centre, and struck with the same radius as
the arch. For the wheel arch, when it passes
throughout the thickness of the wall, it is usual
to fix an upright piece of wood on each side of the
wall, and pass a bar of either wood or iron from
one to the other; this will answer as a centre for
the trammel to swing round upon, either on one
side of the wall or the other.

All joints in good face-work ought to be struck
as full as possible without projecting beyond the
face of the wall, and as straight as the bricks will
allow.

SECTION II.

DRAWING, CUTTING, AND SETTING ARCHES.

It is very necessary, in speaking of arches, that the reader should thoroughly understand what an arch really is. It must not be supposed that any kind of building material which has been used to cover an opening is necessarily an arch simply because it is made to form a curve, for in many cases we see a block of stone cut out in the form of an arch, and placed over doorways, windows, &c. ; but in the centre or crown, where the proper arch is the strongest, the stone being thinnest is the weakest, and being liable to break at any time, causes the work above to give way.

An arch that is perfectly equal may be considered as a slightly elastic curved beam, and, when loaded, every part is in a state of compression. The arch that the bricklayer has to deal with is a quantity of bricks so arranged that they may, by their pressure one upon another, not only support their own weight, but transmit any weight that may be placed on them to the abutments.

Therefore all bricks should be of such a shape that they should "bed" with a perfectly equal bed-joint, one against the other, and at the same time carry an equal curve, or fit the centre upon which the arch is turned, throughout the whole span.

And by each joint cutting in a line to the point or centre from which the arch is struck, each brick will be in the form of a wedge; these are often called " voussoirs," and the thickest or uppermost part of them the " extrados," and the small, or that part which is fixed upon the centre, the "intrados," or soffit of the arch.

These few remarks will serve to clear the mind of the reader as to what the general principles of an arch are.

The higher calculations connected with the designing of arches, and rules to find the weight with which each course of voussoirs should be loaded to bring the arch into perfect equilibrium, would be out of place here, as this little work is intended for the working bricklayer, and he is very seldom fortunate enough to be able to enter into calculations of this kind, although they would be of great service to him.

PLAIN ARCHES.

All arches turned without the bricks being cut or shaped in any way may be classed under this head; and these are in general use for railway-bridges, tunnels, vaultings, and all work where strength is essential, and appearance no particular object.

In building arches of this description, in order to avoid the thick joints that would appear at the extrados if the bricks were laid with the *end* upon the centre—as they are not wedge-shaped, but of one thickness throughout the length—it is usual to build them in rings the thickness of half a brick, or brick on edge, so that each ring is separate, having no connection with the others beyond the cohesion of the mortar in the collar-joints between them, except a heading-course occasionally, whenever the joints of two rings happen to coincide : sometimes this is objected to.

It is very necessary that each ring should be properly bonded throughout the length of the arch, and also that the joints should be of a regular thickness. For if the soffit-ring is built with a thick bed-joint, and the second ring with a thin one, the thick joints will shrink most, thereby causing an unsightly fracture between the two, and so deprive the arch of the strength of the bottom ring.

Mortar made with good lime is considered by many better than cement for this kind of work, for very often cement sets before the work is complete, and any little accident in striking the centres, or from any other cause, is very liable to break the arch.

Let it be here understood that no kind of arch ought to be turned without the centre has *folding wedges*, so as to drop it, when the arch is finished, as easily as possible, and without shaking the arch.

These wedges ought to be drawn a little a day or two before the centres are really struck, so as to give the arch its " bearing."

AXED ARCHES.

These are used very much in the present day, on account of their taking less labour, as it is thought. But it is an inferior sort of work at the best, and often costs as much as gauge-work by the time it is finished.

The bricks of these are simply axed down to a given size, and nothing but the soffits are rubbed; and this is done after they are brought to the required bevel with the hammer boaster and scotch; they are then set in cement, with a joint about three-sixteenths of an inch in thickness, and afterwards pointed.

GAUGE WORK.

This consists of all kinds of work that is cut and brought down to a given gauge upon the rubbing-stone; such as all kinds of arches, mouldings for external cornices, architraves to doorways and windows, eaves, &c., and is considered the most important branch of the trade.

For this purpose a shed should be built to protect the bricks that are to be cut from the wet, and also large enough for the workmen to erect their benches and chopping-blocks to suit their own convenience. They then require the rubbing-stone and a bedding-block. The former ought to be in the form of a circle, and not exceeding 14 inches in diameter; for if it is, it will be very likely to rub out of level on the face, that is, either hollow or cambering; and even with this size it will be found necessary to turn it round in its bed about once a day when in use, for if the stone is unlevel the bricks will assuredly be the same, making very bad work.

The bedding-block is square and of a perfectly smooth surface. It is used for the purpose of scribing and fitting the bricks to the moulds, and

is usually made to the size of one course of the arch,
if double-faced; if not, about 14 by 18 inches.

VARIOUS ARCHES USED IN THE BUILDING TRADE.

It is necessary that the bricklayer should
thoroughly understand the names of all arches
used in the building trade, and also what is
meant by these names. The following are the
principal arches used in building construction :—

The Semi-circular, as shown in Fig. 11.

The Segment, which is the part of a circle only,
as Fig. 12.

Fig. 11.   Fig. 12.

The Camber (Fig. 13).—This arch is a very small
part of a circle, as it is generally reckoned to rise
only one-eighth of an inch to the foot; so if the

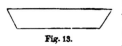

Fig. 13.

span of the arch is four feet,
the crown or centre of the
soffit will only be half an
inch above the springing
line, and the top ought not to be more than a
quarter of an inch above a straight line drawn
from the top of each skewback; then, by the
slight settlement of the arch when taking its
"bearing," this line will have the appearance of
being perfectly straight.

The Gothic Arch (Fig. 14) is very much used
at the present day, both as shown in this figure,

and also with a greater or less rise above the springing line, as Figs. 15 and 16.

The Elliptic Gothic (Fig. 17), which is simply an ellipse with a Gothic head.

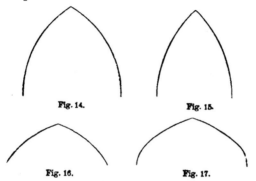

Fig. 14.   Fig. 15.

Fig. 16.   Fig. 17.

Fig. 18 represents a *Semi-ellipse*, or half-oval.

There are many other arches in use in other branches of the building trade; such as the horseshoe (Fig. 19), the O G (Fig. 20). But it

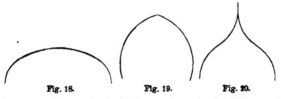

Fig. 18.   Fig. 19.   Fig. 20.

is very seldom the bricklayer has the building of any but those that have been mentioned.

We have thus far only had the forms of different arches. The next thing of importance to the workman is the methods of striking them out, and taking off the moulds and bevels for cutting them.

c 2

DRAWING ARCHES.

As it is out of reason for the builder to pay the workman for his time while he is practising on the work, it will be found necessary that he should learn the different ways of striking out those things that he will require, either at his home, or at some other equally convenient place. And for this purpose he will require a drawing-board. Sixteen inches square will be large enough for this purpose; but should a larger one be required, it would be better to get one 2 ft. 6 in. by 1 ft. 10 in. This will take an imperial sheet of drawing-paper. Also, a T square and setsquare, lead pencils, a pair of compasses with pen and pencil, and a piece of india rubber to clean out any false lines. And as it is always best in these kinds of drawings to work to a scale, the 2-ft. rule will answer this purpose.

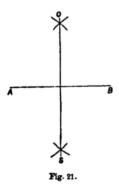

Fig. 21.

Should the reader wish to practise drawing other forms of the arch, he will require more and better instruments.

It is necessary, in almost every kind of arch, to draw the horizontal and perpendicular lines at right angles with one another. If the reader knows how to do this, he will find it his principal guide to drawing the arch.

So, from the points A and B, Fig. 21, with any

radius greater than half the given line A B describe two arcs intersecting each other at o and s;
then the line joining o s will be in the centre of
A B and at right angles with it. But with the
T square and drawing-board this is unnecessary,
as he is simply guided by the square when fixed
first to the side, and then to the bottom of the
board.

In showing the methods of drawing arches and
taking off the moulds, it will not be necessary to
speak of *plain* arches, as the bricks are not cut for
them, therefore it will be best to deal with them
as *gauged*.

The Semi-circular (Fig. 22).—In drawing this
arch, it is only necessary to place one point of the

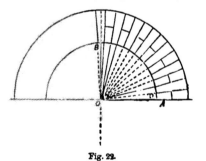

Fig. 22.

compass at the centre o, and with the radius D E
describe the half-circle which will answer for the
soffit; then with the same centre describe a
greater half-circle, according to the depth of the
arch required.

Divide the outer ring with the compass into as

many parts as there are required courses in the arch, taking care to see how thick the bricks will work first, so that no more is wasted in the cutting than necessary. Then from the centre o draw the lines to each of the divisions marked on the outside half-circle as shown. This will be the size and shape of the mould for cutting each course of the face of the arch. And a parallel mould, the width of the *small* end of the face mould, will do for the cutting of the soffit of the brick, after allowing for the joint in each case (this ought to be about one-tenth of an inch thick), and is best done by working a little nearer the small end of the mould, which will be easily seen in the working. The bevel for cutting the soffit is taken by placing the stock of the bevel to the line A, and setting the blade to the line representing the soffit of the first course of the arch at D.

This is the only bevel required (if a T bevel is used) as the tops are cut to this bevel fitted on the brick the reverse way.

Fig. 23 is another kind of semicircular arch with a Gothic head. To draw the outside portion of this arch it is necessary to draw the line or chord A B, bisect it at D, draw a line with the setsquare from D, at right angles with A B, to any point C, and upon this line the centre is taken to describe the outside curve of the arch, according to the haunch required; and the *inner* ring must be divided in the same manner as the *outer* ring of Fig. 22; but the bevels for the tops must be

taken separately. In all other respects it is the
same as Fig. 22.

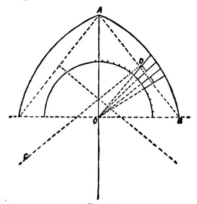

Fig. 23.

The *Segment* (Fig. 24) may be worked in the

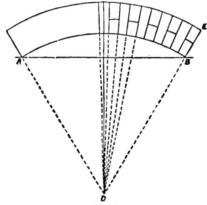

Fig. 24.

same way as the semicircle, the only difference
being in taking the centre to strike it with

This is taken in the perpendicular line below the springing level, with radius according to the rise required as shown at D, and this is the point to which all lines must be drawn, both to get the skewback and also the size of the course. The bevel for cutting the skewback is taken by placing the stock parallel with the springing line A B, and setting the blade of the bevel to the skewback line D E.

We now come to the *Camber Arch*, which is perhaps one of the most difficult to draw and cut. To draw this arch, supposing the opening to be 4 feet in the clear, would require an arch with only half an inch rise above the springing line at the crown, as it would take a very long radius to strike an arch having so small a rise in the ordinary way of striking a *segment* of a circle; it is necessary, therefore, to resort to other means.

To do this it is best, in the first place, to get the horizontal and perpendicular lines, and measure out the width of the opening equal on each side of the upright line, then take the rise as shown at A, Fig. 25, and drive three nails into the board upon which it is intended to strike the arch, at the three separate points B, A, C; this done, get a piece of ½-inch board as long as the opening is wide, in the form of a very flat triangle, as shown in Fig. 26, taking care the rise of the triangle is just half that required for the arch. Place the end B, Fig. 26, to the nail at B, Fig. 25, A to A, and C to C, keeping it tight against A C with the left hand;

then with the right hand fix the pencil firmly
against A, the centre of the trammel, and gently
draw the curve with the right hand, as the
trammel is drawn from A to C with the left. If
care is taken to keep the pencil hard against the
centre A of the trammel, and that part of the

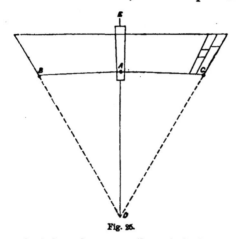

Fig. 25.

trammel against the two nails as it is drawn from
A to C, it will describe very correctly that half of

Fig. 26.

the camber's soffit. Then by repeating the
operation the reverse way, by drawing the
trammel with the left hand from A to B, while
with the right hand and pencil that half is described in like manner, this will complete the
regular curve of the camber arch. Then with

c, as centre, and c b, as radius, cut the perpendicular in d; this is the point to which the lines
are drawn to get the proper skewback.

It is then necessary to measure the bricks to
see how they will work. If 3 inches, set off
1½ inches on each side of the centre line e d,
and draw lines to the point d, as shown: this will
give the shape of the moulds of which there
ought to be three, a quarter of an inch thick, and
about 18 inches in length. If the arch is to be
1 foot in depth, and in proportion if more or less,
then mark them all at about 3 inches from the
narrow end.

Fix one of these upon the centre line, as
shown at a, so the line above mentioned shall be
exactly at the soffit-line of the arch, and then
trace the other two alternately towards the skewback, keeping each line on the moulds to the
soffit-curve each time.

If the last mould does not meet the skewback
exactly, it must be raised or dropped down until
it does; then mark each course, and the joint
must then be allowed as before stated.

The bevels must be taken for *each* course, and
marked on the mould ready for working; one
bevel will answer for *soffit, cross-joint,* and *top* of
each course, if it is reversed for the two last named.
But perhaps it would be best to leave the tops
and cut them when setting the arch, for very
often mistakes are made in taking the length of
the courses with the template. The bond of the
camber arch is the same as the quoin of a

common wall of Flemish bond, only the arch is level and the quoin is upright, always remembering to work from the soffit, as shown by the two courses at c, Fig. 25.

The Gothic Arch (Fig. 26) is much easier to construct than the *camber*, owing to its having a shorter radius.

Set out the extent of the arch at A B on the horizontal line, then with A for centre, and the distance A B for radius, describe the arc C B; then with A E as radius and with the same centre describe

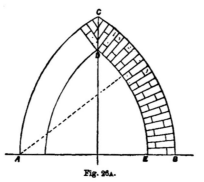

Fig. 26A.

the inner arc D E—this forms one side of the arch; then with B as centre, and same radii used for the first half, describe the second.

Divide the outer curve into courses according to the size of the bricks, and draw the lines to the point A as shown, taking care in dividing out the courses that half a course shall be on each side of the perpendicular line at C, to answer for keybrick. The bevel once set will answer for the

whole of this arch, the same as the semi-circular.
There are different ways of forming the key of
this arch, but the one shown is considered the
best. Sometimes the Gothic arch is cut as repre-
sented in Fig. 27, but it is very seldom, on

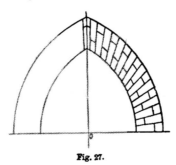

Fig. 27.

account of the extra work in soffiting the bricks,
for in this case each course must be cut to a separate bevel. But the lines for each course are
drawn to the centre o, instead of the opposite
springing, as Fig. 26.

A Reduced or Modified Gothic.—To draw this
arch it is necessary to draw the chords A B and B C,
Fig. 28, from the springing to the crown ; bisect
A B and B C at D and H ; and from these points of
bisection draw the lines to the points o o with the
setsquare. And upon these lines the points are
taken to strike the arch according to the rise
required above the chord. The outer arcs are
then divided into courses and lines drawn to the
points o for the size of the mould, if the arch is
to be cut in the same way as Fig. 26. But if it

is to be "keyed in" with an upright key, as Fig. 27, the lines must be drawn to the centre B.

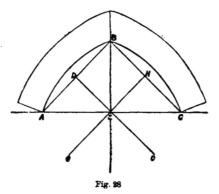

Fig. 28

The method of drawing and taking off the moulds of the arch shown in Fig. 28, applies to any Gothic, whether *greater* or *less* than the regular equilateral arch.

The *Ellipse Gothic* (Fig. 29) is rather more difficult in the working than the generality of Gothic arches, owing to the different striking points. To draw this arch, let the distance A B be set off equally on each side of the perpendicular line ; then divide it into four equal parts by marking the points C D, and with D as centre, and the distance D B as radius, describe the arc from B to E, mark the point B E equal with B D, draw the chord F E, and bisect it at G, from which point draw a line with the setsquare to any point O, and upon this line the centre is taken to draw the upper portion of that side of the arch as shown ;

the soffit curves are obtained in the same way. After the lines A F B B are drawn, they can be made to answer either for *soffit* or *extrados*, by striking the other parts *greater* or *less* than those named ; in this figure they represent the outer

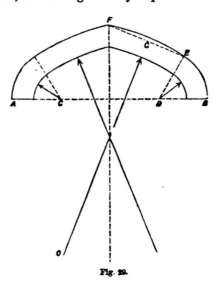

Fig. 29.

ring; but the centres will do for either. The moulds for this arch are taken in the same way as those in the *camber*, Fig. 25; that is, it must be traced over with the moulds, so that each course shall be exactly of one size, and the bevels must be taken separately.

It is of the greatest importance that the workman should practise drawing this arch until he is thoroughly acquainted with every part; for very often he may require quite a different kind of ellipse Gothic to the one here described, and by his understanding the principles of this one he will be better able to reduce or elevate them to suit his requirements. Perfect accuracy in all good brickwork cannot be too much impressed upon the mind of the bricklayer, and more particularly in drawing and cutting arches.

Fig. 30 represents a *semi-ellipsis* arch, and is a great deal like the ellipse Gothic, the only dif-

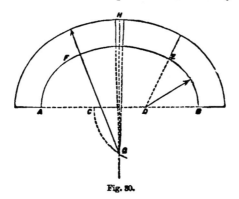

Fig. 30.

ference being in the crowns. But the drawing is quite different. In drawing this arch, divide the span into three equal parts, as shown at A C D B, then, with D as centre and D B for radius, describe the arc from B to E equal to D B, and the same on the opposite side to F; then, with D for centre and the distance D C for radius, describe an arc cutting the perpendicular line in G; and from this point, with the distance G F, describe the arc F E: the

outer curves are taken from the same centres.
The moulds for this arch must be traced in the
same way as the *camber* and ellipse Gothic; that
is, take the thickness of the brick and set it equally
on each side of the centre line at H, as shown;
then draw the lines to G; this will give the size
of the mould very nearly; then, if they are worked
alternately down to the springing-line, it will be
seen where they want easing, should they require
it. The bevels are all taken separately for each
course, but the T bevel reversed will not answer
for the top or outer curve of this arch.

Another method of drawing this arch is shown
in Fig. 31. Take the distance A B, that is, the

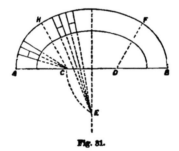

Fig. 31.

span and also the *depth* of the arch, and set it off
equal on each side of the centre line; divide
this into three equal parts by marking the points
c and D; then, with D as centre and D c for radius,
describe an arc cutting the upright line in E. From
this point draw a straight line through D to any
point F, and another through c to H; then with D
as centre and D B for radius describe the arc F B, and

take c for centre and same radius for the opposite
ellipse A H, and, lastly, E for centre and E H for
radius, to describe the crown H F. The soffit-ring
is drawn from the same points. It is thought by
some that the moulds can be taken by drawing
lines as shown from divisions on the outer curves;
but it is evident the bricks in the arch cannot be
all of one size and shape if this is done, although
there is little doubt the arch is stronger that way,
owing to there being a better skewback at H and F
for the crown than there would be if each course
were cut to one mould; it is unnecessary to say
this is the easiest method. But the appearance is
not so good, for it is an understood thing in the
trade that all courses of an arch should be of one
size.

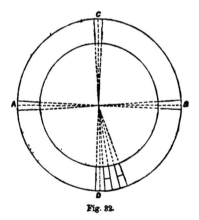

Fig. 32.

The Wheel Arch, or Bull's-eye (Fig. 32).—In
this arch the outer circle is divided out in such a

manner that each line, A B, C D, shall be in the
centre of the course; or, in other words, that
each of these points shall show a key brick, in
the same way as one key is shown in the semi-
circular arch.

Where two or more arches are set close together, "saddles" ought always to be cut, as
shown at A and B (Fig. 33), and not a continual

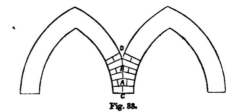

Fig. 33.

straight joint from C to D; for although this is
often done, there is no bond between the two
arches. In all arch cutting the $\top$ bevel is by far
the best to use, for by reversing, it frequently
answers the purpose of two.

MOULDING.

It has been already stated that moulding is
also included in what is called gauge-work. And
of late years there has been a very great deal
of this work done, particularly in and about
London. St. Pancras Station of the Midland
Railway may be taken as a fine specimen.

In many places this is done by simply making
a template the form of the brick required, and
marking the brick, first on one side and then on

the other, and so cutting or rubbing it down to these marks. But for moulding birds' mouths, splay, bulls' noses, and, in fact, almost any kind of work, it will be found much better if a box is made that will hold three or four bricks, either flat or on edge, as they may be required, taking care that the ends are both alike, and the exact shape of the brick required. If this method be properly worked it will be found very accurate, and done with a great deal less labour. The boxes for this purpose are usually covered with tin or sheet-iron to protect the wood from wearing away while working the bricks; if not, the moulds are very apt to get out of their proper shape and so lead the workman wrong. Even with this precaution, it is very necessary to try them sometimes to see if they are correct.

When bricks are moulded for arches, it is best to mould them *first* and cut them to the shape required afteawards; for should they be cut first and then moulded the brick is often broken, and all the labour upon it is wasted.

But it must be remembered that when the bricks are moulded first the soffit is not touched afterwards, or otherwise the bead, or splay, or whatever it is, will be rubbed out of shape. Therefore the brick must be brought down to the required bevel by rubbing down the side or "bed," so as to bring it thinner at the soffit end. This is called soffiting the brick from the side; and all bricks properly worked this way will go together equally as well as if they were bevelled from the end, in the same way as arches that are *not* moulded.

It has been said that where a great many arches are required, all of one size, either *plain* or moulded, it is best to send the moulds to the brickyard and have them cut while the earth is soft, and so burnt to the shape required. But if this is tried it will prove a total failure, for it is impossible to burn bricks with the accuracy required for gauge work; and it is always found to take almost as much labour in bringing them to proper order as it would have done to cut the bricks in the proper manner at first.

Let the bricklayer be careful to turn out his work in such a way that it shall reflect credit upon himself, and his employer will soon see which is the best and cheapest method of cutting gauge-work.

SETTING.

It has already been said that cutting is considered the most important branch of the trade, and to a great extent this is right. But it must be remembered that, after the work is cut, there is almost as much skill required in setting it. For it very often happens that a vast amount of labour and skill is expended upon work while in the "cutter's" hands, and directly it is taken on to the building the beauty of it is all destroyed through the carelessness or inability of the setter. On the contrary, bad cut work is often made to look well through nothing but the skill of the setter.

Therefore it is very necessary that this branch should be equally well understood. In setting gauge-work of all kinds, it is necessary to take the thickness of the courses, and gauge the centre upon which the arch is to be turned; and this is done by taking the thickness of the brick and joint at the soffit. Each course should be marked on the centre from the key brick downwards. Never gauge from the springing or the skewback, as this often leads to mistakes when setting the arch.

The soffit of each course ought to fit the centre perfectly; and in order that it should do so and that the courses should come in right at the key. it is often necessary to have a radius line; that is, a nail should be driven into the ledge of the centre at the point o (Fig. 23), for instance, and a piece of string fastened to it, and drawn up to each course of the arch as it is set, in the same manner as the line o D is drawn. This will prevent the setter getting his work too high or too low at the extrados of the arch. If this is not done he is working at random, and will very likely have to make his bricks smaller, or, other-wise, his bed-joint thicker when he gets to the key; thereby depriving the arch of its strength, and so causing a settlement when the centres are struck. Gauged arches, as a rule, are set in grey lime putty, brought to the consistence of cream. This is put into an oblong wooden box, about 2 ft. by 1 ft. 9 in. deep, for the setter to dip that side of the brick where the bed-joint is required.

But in doing this care must be taken that the bricks are neither too wet nor too dry; also that the putty is of such a thickness that it will give the brick just such a joint as the work requires: of course the brick should be held in the putty until it takes up the joint. If each course is bedded regularly throughout its thickness, the joint will be full and even on the face of the arch; and should it project a little, which is often the case, it ought to be left until the building is cleaned down, then they can be rubbed off level with the bricks, and so leave the face of the arch perfectly regular. This method only applies to gauge-work.

Axed Work

Is usually set in Portland cement; and this is sometimes mixed with a little putty to make it work better; the brick is then "buttered" with the trowel and not dipped as gauge-work. By being buttered is meant a small portion of the cement drawn on the edges of the brick, and the middle left hollow to receive the cement grout which is run in after the work is set; the joints are then raked out to receive the tuck pointing, which is done after the building is up. Whenever there is a long range of arches, *one* ought not to be set separately; but a line drawn the whole length, so that when all are set, they shall be perfectly straight one with another.

SECTION III.

DIFFERENT KINDS OF POINTING.

POINTING of all kinds of work is another very important branch which the bricklayer has to deal with, and is more in practice at the present day than ever before, both on account of its cheapness and also its appearance. These may be classed under two heads—*Tuck-pointing* and flat-joint pointing. The first is of the most importance, and also requires the most skill, not only in the different methods of preparing and using the material, but also in preparing the work.

Stock work with the white joint is most general in London; and the first thing necessary is to mix the pointing stuff. It is often thought best to colour the work, even if it is a new building, to bring all the bricks to a uniform colour, because some bricks are much darker than others, and therefore have a bad appearance when finished. This colour as a rule is made with green copperas in the proportion of one pound of copperas to five gallons of water; but in all cases it should be tried first upon some bricks placed in the same position as the front which is to be coloured; that is, if the front face the south, place the bricks towards the same quarter, as it is often found that work dried in the sun, and that which is dried in the shade, are quite different

Mix up as much colour as will complete the whole job, as two mixings might not be alike. The longer this copperas is kept the stronger it gets; therefore if it cannot all be used at once, it is best to weaken it every morning by putting half a pint of water to every gallon of colour; if this is not looked to, the last part which is done will be much darker than the first. If the work is wetted before the colour is laid on, one gallon of colour will do 100 feet, more or less, according to the bricks and the season of the year.

Yellow Stopping.—This is made with grey lime, putty, and fine washed sand, in the proportion of one bushel of the former to three of the latter, and will take about 2 lbs. of yellow ochre to each hodful of stopping. But of course the workman will regulate it to suit the colour of the brick. This also must be tried in the same way as the copperas, and in all cases let the stopping be a shade darker than the brick when it is dry. This will give the putty joint a better appearance when it is laid on. In no case should copperas be used to colour the stopping.

White Putty.—This is generally made with chalk lime (because it dries much whiter than grey lime, and gives the work a better appearance), and silversand, or marble dust; the latter should be used whenever it can be obtained, on account of its giving the joint a beautiful glaze. It is usual to heat the pieces of marble until they fall to a powder, then screen it through a very fine screen or sieve before mixing it with the lime. But silver sand is more generally used.

The lime is slaked and sifted through a fine sieve. Sometimes oil or size is mixed with it to make it work better, and also to give it greater binding properties; but this must be done while the lime is hot and dry, and one pint of either to half a bushel of lime is enough.

If chalk lime is used, one peck of silver sand is sufficient for half a bushel of lime; but if grey lime is used, it will take double that quantity of sand. If work is to be pointed, it must be well cleaned down from top to bottom, and well rubbed with pieces of the same brick as the wall is built with; this will give the work a level surface. Brush off all dust, and wet it well, then follow with the colour and give it one coat throughout; if it should require two coats, let one get well set before the second is laid on; but if it only requires one coat, the work is ready for the stopping. It is usual to do this in lengths of about 8 feet; this is about the length that two men will work when laying on the fine stuff; and if this is taken for the length and 5 feet for the height, it will be quite enough at one time.

We sometimes see houses stopped in from top to bottom before ever a putty joint is laid on; but the man who does this evidently knows but very little about tuck-pointing, for, whenever this is done, the stopping gets so dry and hard that the putty will not combine with it as it ought, and it will fall off in a very short time,

The work is also so besmeared with the white stuff, that it has more the appearance of being plastered than tuck-pointed.

When the length, as before stated, is stopped in, it is usual to rub it well with a piece of dry sacking, or something of that kind, to give the stopping and bricks the appearance of being one uniform block. Brush off all dust, and, if necessary, damp it with the stock-brush carefully, so as not to disturb the stopping; then gauge the joints at each end of the rule as a guide for holding it, so that each course is of the same thickness, and each joint perfectly level throughout. This gauging must be applied to all work, whether yellow, white, or red, and it would be best to have a gauge-rod expressly for this purpose. The cross-joints should be perfectly plumb from top to bottom of the building. The rule that is used to lay on the bed-joints (if it is done with the jointers) is about 8 feet long, 5 inches wide, and about $\frac{1}{2}$ inch thick; and there ought to be two or three pieces of cork a quarter of an inch thick nailed on to the back, to keep the rule from the work, so as to allow room for the waste putty that is cut from the joint to fall clear to the ground. The fine stuff is spread upon this rule, and afterwards taken off it with the jointer and laid on the work that is stopped in, according to the rule when it is held to the gauge-marks. After this the rough edges are cut off with a knife, or "Frenchman," as it is called. This is the process for yellow or stock-work pointing.

Red brickwork is treated in many respects quite differently. The colour used for this is composed of 1 lb. of Venetian red, and 1 lb. of Spanish brown to 1½ gallons of water; but it ought to be tried in the same way as copperas. This colour has no setting properties, therefore it is necessary to mix something with it that has, or else the first shower of rain will surely wash it off.

One of the best things to use for this purpose is white copperas. This must be dissolved in warm water, and 1 lb. will set about 3 gallons of colour. Alum is also used in the same proportions; and sometimes half a gallon of stale beer to the same quantity of colour for setting.

Red Stopping is composed of 1 part of grey lime to 3 parts of fine washed sand (red sand would be better, as it would take less colouring). This is coloured with Venetian red and a small portion of vegetable black. But in this case no proportions can be given as there are so many different kinds of red brick, and the colour that would suit one would look very badly if applied to another; therefore it is best for the workman to try these colours, and match them with the bricks before he begins to point the real work, and in all cases mix enough for the whole of the pointing, allowing three hods of stopping to 200 feet of work.

This class of work is done in the same way as stock-work, the only difference being in the using the colour. Red work is coloured throughout first, and then a second coat is laid on *after it has been stopped;* this is done very lightly, so as not to rub up the stopping.

But in stock-work, colouring over the stopping should never be done, for the copperas being so strong it will bring out a white hue, and make the stopping almost as white as the putty joint, giving the whole of the work a very bad appearance. The putty for red work is just the same as that used for stock-work.

White Brickwork.—When the bricks used for this work are sand-made, they only require well rubbing down before pointing; but should there be any flesh-coloured ones among them, it is best to leave the dust on the face after rubbing it, and give the whole a coat of alum-water; this will set the dust so securely on the face of the bricks, that no quantity of water will wash it off, and will give the whole front a regular appearance. This is made with 1 lb. of alum dissolved in 3 gallons of hot water; and if it can be laid on the work when warm, so much the better.

The stopping for this kind of work seldom wants any colouring, the sand making it sufficiently dark to match the bricks.

There are three sorts of putty used for this work; white, black, and sometimes red.

The method of mixing the first has already been explained, therefore it is unnecessary to repeat it.

Black Putty requires $\frac{1}{2}$ bushel of grey lime, slaked and finely sifted; $1\frac{1}{2}$ bushels of very fine washed, or silver sand   and 12 lbs. of lamp-black or vegetable black: the last named is much easier to mix with the lime and sand. Care must be taken that these are well worked into one another, if not, the joint will have a bad appearance when laid on the work.

Red Putty.—This is made in the same way as the black, only the colouring is different, this being done with Spanish brown. But, as in red stopping, the colour must be mixed to the shade required.

It is not always necessary to colour brickwork; and if the bricks are all of one colour, such as Suffolk whites, best reds, or malms, it is much better not to do so.

But if, on the contrary, the bricks are inferior, they cannot be brought to a uniform colour without it.

The putty-joint in all tuck-pointing ought not to exceed a quarter of an inch in thickness. Arches of all kinds, except those that are gauged, are pointed in the same way as plain brickwork, but the joint ought to be smaller.

Old Brickwork.—When this is repointed all the old mortar must be raked out of the joints. The whole front is then well rubbed with pieces of brick to clean off the grease and dirt, and well swept down with a hard broom perfectly clean, so that the colour may enter the face of the brick, and after this, it is given two coats of red colour or green copperas as the case may be, taking care that the first coat is dry before the second is laid on, also that both are dry before it is stopped in.

The stopping in old work is generally smoothed down level with the face of the bricks with the trowel, and not rubbed in the way that new work usually is; for very often it is stopped with brown or black stopping, if it is stockwork, and, of course, it would never do to rub it.

Flat-joint Pointing.—This is of three kinds. The first is laid on with the trowel and cut off at the top only with the Frenchman, to give the joint the appearance of having been struck when the bricks were laid. The second kind is cut off top and bottom, and is sometimes called "half-tuck." And the third is simply done by filling up each joint flush with the brick; then rub it over with a stock-brush or a piece of sacking, and next run a line in the centre with a jointer or anything that will mark it. Inside work which is to be whitewashed or coloured is the only work which is done with this kind of pointing. Washed sand and lime made into a stiff mortar is the only pointing material required for flat-joint pointing, but the darker the sand the better, and in this case, as in all kinds of pointing, the work should be kept well damped, for upon this depends the soundness of the pointing.

SECTION IV.

PAVING, TILING, USE OF MATERIALS, ETC.

—

PAVING.

Brick-paving.—This kind of flooring is less used in London than it is in the country, as it is often the practice to lay the floors of dwelling-houses in many parts with this material; but this is seldom done in the metropolis, unless it is the cellar floors, and these are usually done with the stockbricks; good paviours and Dutch clinkers being used only for stables, coach-houses, &c. These are laid in various ways, such as brick-flat, brick-on-edge, and sometimes it is herringboned.

Plain Paving is that which is laid in parallel courses. This needs no explanation further than

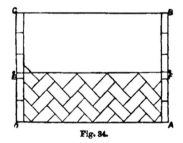

Fig. 34.

that which will be given in connection with the other kinds. But herringbone paving, Fig. 34, will be found much more difficult, both in setting out and also after it is set out, in the working.

The first thing that must be done is to get the floor-line, at any point such as A, and, if necessary, drive a stake into the ground as a starting-point to take the levels from. From this point level to each corner of the room, taking care to reverse the level every length, for very often the level is not correct, and the work is thereby thrown out. But if this is done it cannot happen. After the levels are taken, the ground must be dug out deep enough to receive the brick and its bed below the level line; if this is *brick-flat*, 3 inches will be enough, but if *on edge*, it will take 5 inches; then with a pair of lines lay a temporary course of brick, as shown from D to c and from A to B, and the line is drawn to these courses to keep the work level on the surface and also to show if the points of the herringbone are correct, as shown by the line E F. No bricks ought to be cut against the straight temporary courses, but leave them as a toothing to be filled up afterwards. All diagonal joints should cut in a line, in the same way as those explained in Figs. 7 and 8, and those figures will serve for a guide for *brick-on-edge* paving, Fig. 34 representing *brick-flat* only. But the straight temporary courses are laid for all sorts of brick paving.

Tile-paving is very much in practice, both plain and ornamental, notwithstanding the great quantities of asphalte Portland cement and York paving used. These tiles vary in thickness from two inches to three-eighths of an inch. Plain tiling is generally done with tiles, 12, 9, and

6 inches square; and these are laid in parallel courses with one side of the room, yard, or surface that requires paving. Should the tiles be of different colours, it is usual to lay them diagonally, so that the different colours form diamonds. The methods of executing this kind of paving are much the same as the others. But for very thin or ornamental tiling the whole surface is "screeded" perfectly level with Portland cement mixed with sand; and when sufficiently hard, the tiles are laid with a thin bed of pure cement, according to a design; by frequently applying the straight-edge, the work will be brought to a uniform surface.

TILING.

Roofing-tiles.—These are of two kinds, *plain tiles,* which are quite flat, with two holes near the head of the tile, through which oak pins are placed, and by this means the tiles are laid or hung to the laths of the roof; and *pantiles,* which are much larger. These are hollow, or curve-shaped, and are hung on the laths with a projecting ear, which is called the nob of the tile; and each course overlaps the previous one with a roll. This tiling is done much better in the country than in London, owing, in a great measure, to the tiles being made with greater care, and better shaped. If this work is properly gauged, the courses ought to fit perfectly close one to the other, so as to prevent the wind getting under them and lifting them off.

In preparing the roof for tiling, it is necessary to lath it with inch laths. These are called *pantile laths*. To do this, each outside rafter (that is, the rafter that is nearest to each gable) should be gauged out according to the gauge of the tiles. This is done from the *eaves* to the *ridge*, taking care to allow for the eaves projecting over the wall-plates, so as to carry off the water. This is easily ascertained by fitting a tile on to the eaves before gauging the roof. Nails are then temporarily driven into the rafter at each length of the gauge, and to these nails a line is drawn, as a guide line for lathing the roof.

Where these tiles are used for dwelling houses, each space between the pantile laths is covered with small laths, and these are covered with a bed of mortar, to answer for a bed for the tile, and also to keep out the wind; but in common tiling this is not done, as pointing the tiles inside answers much the same purpose. The roof ought to be gauged out lengthways also, the width of each course, so as to finish exactly even courses at the gable. For not unfrequently we see roofs covered at random, and finished with a broken or cut course against the gable, and this will generally be found to be the first place where the water penetrates through, thereby causing a great deal of injury to the roof, ceilings, &c.

Plain Tiling is worked much in the same way; but of course the gauge is less. They are sometimes hung with two little nobs instead of pins. In plain tiling, the roof needs only to be gauged

from the eaves to the ridge; the guide lengthways is simply to keep the second course half
bond on the first, and so on throughout the roof.
The setting of ridge-tiles needs no explanation,
as it is only necessary to keep them level and
straight along the ridge-tree; the different gauges
will be given further on.

It is the practice in buildings of any importance to construct fireproof floors, and this is

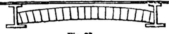

Fig. 35.

sometimes done by turning brick arches upon
wrought iron girders as shown in Fig. 35. But
of late years it has been found that plain tiles
will answer this purpose equally as well as bricks,
without the disadvantage of being so heavy. Not
only that, but the depth of the girder can be
greatly reduced, for often where a 6-inch girder
would be required for brick arches, those 3 inches
in depth would do for tiles, so saving the 3 inches
in the thickness of the flooring. And not only
fireproof floors, but many flat roofs have been
covered with two or three courses of tiles, either

Fig. 36.

laid flat upon the girders, as shown in Fig. 36,
or arched as Fig. 35; but by all means let them
break joint. The tiles should be well wetted,
and the finer the sand used with the cement for

bedding them the better. This construction of floors, &c., although appearing very slight, will carry an immense weight, if the cement used is of good quality.

SCAFFOLDING.

One of the principal things necessary to the carrying out of a building is the scaffolding, and great care ought to be taken in selecting the men that are to do it, for upon their care and foresight often depends the lives of the other men engaged on the work. Scaffolding in general use for brickwork consists of standards, ledgers, putlogs, and boards. The standards and ledgers are of fir, and of various lengths up to 50 feet, and are about 7 inches diameter at the butt end. Foreign poles are much better adapted for scaffolding than English, on account of their freedom from knots, and their being thinner according to the length. Putlogs are usually made of birch 4 inches square by 6 feet in length. Cords and wedges are used to fasten the standards, ledgers, and putlogs in their proper places. Standards are placed upright about 5 feet from the wall and 10 feet apart throughout the length of the building.

The ledgers are tied up horizontally to the standards to support the putlogs; these are placed crossways with one end resting on the ledger, and the other in the wall, and upon these putlogs the boards are laid to complete the scaffold; the latter are of different lengths up to

14 or 16 feet; in no case should scaffolding be used if it is rotten, or likely to break; it sometimes happens that the butts are decayed a little and the other parts of the pole perfectly sound; in this case it is best to cut off the bad part. The standards should be let into the ground about two feet, and the earth firmly rammed round them, to keep them upright; and where the soil is soft, pieces of brick or stones should first be rammed in the bottom of the hole, to keep the pole from settling down when the scaffold is loaded; for should the poles sink the putlogs will act as levers and overturn the wall.

When one length of poles is not sufficient, two are lashed together, top and butt, and diagonal braces are then fixed, to prevent the scaffold from moving in any way.

RELIEVING ARCHES.

All openings in walls for doorways, windows, &c., where wood lintels are used as attachments for internal fittings, should be arched over with relieving arches throughout the whole thickness of the wall. And the springing of such arches ought always to be beyond the end of the lintel. If beams of any kind or joists are to be built into the walls, it is best to leave recesses for the timber, so that the brickwork is not built upon it, as it is liable to lead to settlements, and frequently the cause of the fronts of houses being bulged out just where the joist runs into the inside of the wall.

When iron girders enter brick walls to support

fireproof floors, iron bressummers (to support the other work over shop fronts, &c.), York stone templates are bedded in the wall for the ends of the girders to rest upon, so as to distribute the weight over as large a bearing-area as possible.

BAKERS' OVENS.

To construct a baker's oven to heat with coals : the size of the base having been arranged, it should be carried up to the height of the furnace door, and the ashpit left according to the width of the door and the length of the furnace-bars, allowing for the door being set $4\frac{1}{2}$ inches from the face of the brickwork. Let the frame and door be about a foot square, like the furnace-door of a copper, and the bars about 20 inches long, and level with the bottom of the oven and of the door. Let the flue be about 16 inches square, for the fire to shoot into the oven from the shoulder where the furnace is straight across to the opposite angle of the oven, and by the fire catching the crown in its course it will spread all round. Let a register be fixed in the flue, and the copper five or six inches above the furnace, not so as to get too hot, for it is usually *warm* water only that is required in a bakehouse. A register should be fixed within a little of where the flue enters the oven, and rise slanting ; which, being stopped when the oven is hot enough, leads into the chimney flue. The general rise of the crown above the floor is from 18 to 20 inches. Sometimes the oven is constructed without the copper. And perhaps it is the best plan; for it is certain the two will act better apart than they do together; but of course the latter is a little the cheapest as regards fuel.

But in building ovens, as well as many other things, the work is done according to the situation and the owner's convenience. At all events, the side walls, from which the crown of the oven springs, ought not to be less than $2\frac{1}{2}$ bricks thick, and the crown springing from about 9 inches above the floor. The angles should all intersect, and all be laid with as close joint as possible.

When the oven is "domed," spread some sand on the top, so that when the work gets dry the sand may fill up any cracks.

SMOKY CHIMNEYS.

The causes of these are so various, that it is impossible to lay down any general rule as a cure. But perhaps the following remarks may be found useful :—

The evil is generally in the construction. The flues are often too large or too small, or otherwise the chimney-shaft is not carried up high enough to prevent the wind from blowing over the roofs adjoining, and so the smoke is prevented from rising. And again, it is not unfrequently we see pots placed upon the chimneys of a house all of a uniform size and shape. It matters not whether the flue leads from a drawing-room fire or a kitchen, while perhaps the latter produces nearly double the smoke of the former; the result is, the kitchen chimney smokes, owing to the flue being cramped up at the top. Another cause of kitchen chimneys smoking, is when other flues are connected with them; for instance, when cooking apparatus is fixed in a kitchen, it is thought well to connect the flue with the flue from the kitchen-range; and this is usually done about 2 or 3 feet above the fire-place. This may answer very well if the two are always in use at the same time. But, should the kitchen fire alone be required, it is very likely the cold air from the flue of the apparatus will enter straight into the kitchen-flue, just at the entrance of the shaft, and prevent the smoke from rising.

The author has proved the whole of these evils, and therefore knows them to exist.

No chimney-flue of a dwelling-house ought to be less than 9 inches by 14; and the kitchen flue ought to be 14 inches square throughout the entire length of the chimney.

The shaft ought to be carried up above the highest part of the roof; and if chimney-pots are used, they ought to be all of one height, and *the area of the end of the pot equal the top of the flue.* In building the flues, turn them first one way and then the other, so as to prevent the rain from falling down the chimney, and also to give it a sharper draught. But care must be taken that the flues have the same room for the smoke.

To Proportion Windows to Rooms.

To give the proper light, neither too much nor too little, multiply the length of the room by the breadth, and that product by the height, and out of this extract the square root, which root will be the space to give the proper light for the room, and may be divided into as many windows as the room will allow.

Suppose the room to be 22 feet long by 18 feet wide, the product will be 396, and multiplied by the height, 11 feet, the product will be 4,356, whose square root is 66, which will be the area of light space of the room, and may be divided into 3 windows of 22 feet each. This is thought to be the best rule for the purpose.

Materials, their Use, etc.

A rod of brickwork laid 4 courses to 11½ inches requires 4,530 stock bricks.

A rod of brickwork laid 4 courses to the foot, 4,350 bricks.

N.B.—420 stocks weigh about 1 ton, and 460 go to a cubic yard. Sometimes the number of bricks to a rod of brickwork will be 4,500 allowing for waste, and the amount of lime and sand to equal the above would be about 22 bushels of the former to 77 of the latter.

But, of course, this is beyond what it really takes for ordinary buildings; but some require a great deal more cutting, and so a greater quantity

of bricks are spoiled.   For dwelling-houses, &c.,
4,300 to a rod is sufficient.

If laid dry, 5,370 bricks to the rod.

And in wells and circular cesspools, 4,900.

Should there be any odd feet in the calculations
for buildings in general, it is usual to reckon 16
bricks to the foot standard thickness.

A rod of brickwork, laid 4 courses to the foot,
contains 235 cubic feet of bricks and 71 cubic feet
of mortar, and weighs about 14½ tons; but, of
course, this depends upon the bricks, whether
they are wet or dry.

A rod of brickwork measures 16½ feet square,
1½ bricks thick (which is called the reduced or
standard thickness), or 272 feet 3 inches superficial; or 306 cubic feet, or 11½ cubic yards.
These are the measurements in general use.   But
sometimes 18 feet are allowed to the rod, that is,
324 square feet; and also the rod of 21 feet long
and 3 feet high, that is 63 square feet.   In this
case no regard is paid to the thickness of the wall
in measuring.   But the price is regulated according to the thickness.

Nevertheless, all calculations in this little work
will be to the rod of 272 feet 3 inches.

A rod of brickwork requires 1½ cubic yards of
chalk lime and 3 single loads of sand, or one
cubic yard of *grey* lime and 3½ loads of sand, or
24 bushels of Portland cement and 48 bushels of
sharp sand.

A cubic yard of mortar requires 7 bushels of
grey lime and 23 bushels of sand.

Lime and sand and also cement and sand lose one-third of their bulk when made up into mortar; therefore the proportion of mortar or cement when made up is to the lime and sand or cement and sand, as when dry, 2 to 3.

Lime or cement and sand to make mortar require as much water as equals one-third of their bulk.

A standard yard of brickwork laid 4 courses to the foot, requires $\frac{3}{4}$ bushel of cement and $1\frac{1}{2}$ bushel of sand and 150 bricks.

One barrel of cement, containing 5 bushels, cask included, weighs about $3\frac{3}{4}$ hundreds.

A yard of 9-inch wall requires $\frac{1}{2}$ bushel of cement, 1 bushel of sand, and 100 stock bricks.

$4\frac{1}{2}$-inch facing requires 7 bricks per superficial foot.

$4\frac{1}{2}$-inch gauged-work requires 10 bricks per superficial foot.

Brick nogging per yard superficial requires 30 bricks on edge, or 47 laid flat.

30 hods of mortar equal one load.

A measure of lime is 27 cubic feet, and contains 21 striked bushels.

27 cubic feet, or one cubic yard, is called a single load; and two cubic yards a double load.

A hundred of lime is 25 bushels.

The weight of a bushel of well-burnt chalk lime is from 36 to 38 lbs.; and grey stone lime from 46 to 59 lbs.

Paving with bricks or tiles requires 1 yard of

sand to every 12 yards, or if laid and grouted in with mortar, 1½ bushels of lime and 4 bushels of sand to 12 yards.

Stock brick, flat paving, requires 36 per yard super.

,,	on edge	,, 52	,,
Paving bricks, laid flat		,, 36	,,
,,	on edge	,, 82	,,
Dutch clinkers, laid flat		,, 70	,,
,,	on edge	,, 140	,,
12-inch paving tiles		,, 9	,,
10-inch	,,	,, 13	,,
6-inch	,,	,, 36	,,

Tiling. Description.	Gauge in inches.	Number required per square.
With pantiles . . .	12 . . .	150
,, . . .	11 . . .	160
,, . . .	10 . . .	180
With plain tiles . .	4 . . .	600
,, . .	3½ . . .	700
,, . .	3 . . .	800

N.B.—These figures are quite near enough as regards quantities; but as a rule the tiles are tried before the roof is lathed, to find the correct gauge, as they are of various shapes and sizes.

A square of pan tiling requires 2 bundles of 5 ft. laths, and 1,000 of sixpenny nails, if small lathed.

A square of plain tiling requires about 1 bundle of oak laths, 5 score to the bundle, 5 feet long—if 4 feet long there is 6 score, and if 3 feet long, 8 score, to the bundle; 450 nails; 3 hods of mortar, or lime and hair; and, if the tiles are hung with pins, between half a peck and a peck will be required; oak pins are those usually used.

All pantiling is executed by working from the eaves to the ridge each course, and from the right-hand end of the roof to the left. But plain tiles are hung in horizontal courses the whole length of the roof from right to left.

Flat plain tiling for floors, flat roofs, &c., if

two courses thick, 420 tiles, 3 bushels of Portland cement, and 6 bushels of sharp washed sand for a square superficial; and 210 tiles, 1½ bushels of cement, and 3 bushels of sand for every extra course.

A measure, yard, or load, of lime, sand, or earth is 27 cubic feet or 21 striked bushels.

A chaldron is 41 cubic feet, and contains 32 bushels.

A labourer's hod measures 1 foot 4 inches by 9 inches by 9, and will hold 14 bricks, or three-quarters of a cubic foot of mortar or cement.

The following is a table of sizes and weights of various articles used by the bricklayer :—

Description.	Length.		Breadth.		Thick-ness.		Weight.	
	ft.	in.	ft.	in.	ft.	in.	lbs.	ozs.
Stock bricks, each . .	0	9	0	4½	0	2½	5	4
Paving „ „ . .	0	9	0	4½	0	1½	4	0
Dutch clinkers, each .	0	6½	0	3	0	1½	1	8
12-in. paving tiles, each	0	11½	0	11½	0	1½	13	0
10-in. „ „	0	9½	0	9½	0	1½	9	0
9-in. „ „	0	8½	0	8½	0	1½	7	5
Pantiles, each . . .	1	2½	0	9½	0	0½	5	4
Plain tiles, each . . .	0	11	0	6½	0	0½	2	5
Pantile laths per 10 ft. bundle	120	0	0	1½	0	1	4	6
Ditto per 12 ft. bundle (N.B.—A bundle contains 12 laths.)	144	0	0	1½	0	1	5	0
Plain tile laths per bundle . . . . . (30 bundles 1 load.)	500	0	0	1	0	0¼	0	12

A square of pantiling requires 1 bundle of pantile laths 12 feet long, and 144 2-inch nails.

SECTION V.

SLATER AND PLASTERER'S WORK.

In many parts of the country the slater's business,
&c., is done by the bricklayer. And where such is
the case, all materials for shelves, cisterns, baths,
lavatories, &c., are worked by the stone mason;
for, as a rule, there is not sufficient work in small
towns to keep a slater exclusively for that business, and in many country towns and villages
slates are not used for anything but the covering
of roofs. As a general rule, all men in the building trade understand what tools the slater uses,
and also what they are used for; therefore it is
quite unnecessary to describe them.

It is best in all cases, if possible, that the quantity of slates required for the roof should be
brought to the building before the slater begins
to work; then he will see the whole of them, and
sort them out accordingly: this is done by dividing the slates into three thicknesses,—these are
thicks, middlings, and thins; this is done so that
the thickest slates should be at the bottom, the
middling ones next, and the thinnest nearest the
ridge; it is also essential to the soundness as well
as the appearance of slating. After this they are
all dressed to one size, and the edges trimmed
perfectly straight, gauged, and the holes made.

The upper surface of a slate is called its back;
the under surface the bed; the top edge the head;

and the bottom the tail; that part of the slate which is exposed to view when hung, the "margin" of the course; and the width of the margin is the gauge; the "lap" is that distance by which the tail of the third course overlaps the head of the first, as shown in Fig. 37.   In some

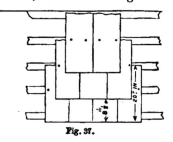

Fig. 37.

cases the slate is fastened with the nails driven as near the head as possible; but it will be found much better, both for the soundness and also appearance, if the nails for the second course are driven in just above the head of the first, because if the slate is fastened with the nails near the middle, it is evident the wind cannot have the leverage that it would if it were fastened at the head.   The gauge of all kinds of slates used for covering roof will be equal to half the distance from the tail to the head, less the lap.   For instance, suppose the lap to be 2 inches, and a countess slate 20 inches from tail to head, first deduct 2 inches, the lap, from 20 inches, the length, of the slate, this leaves 18 inches; half 18 inches is therefore the gauge of a countess slate with a 2-inch lap.

After the slates are gauged, perhaps it would be best to lay one of them on the roof at the eaves, letting it project over for the drip, according to arrangement—this is generally about 3 inches; and by so doing it will easily be seen where the first lath should be nailed on the rafters, and from the top of the first lath to the top of the second, and so on, is the gauge. The first lath at the eaves ought to be a little thicker than the others, so as to give the first course of slates its springing; and the ends of the lath, at the gables, ought also to be raised up about three-eighths of an inch to throw the water off; if not, it will frequently soak between the cement fillets or under the lead flushing and so enter the roof.

All slating laths should be from two to three inches wide and five-eighths of an inch thick. The nails used should be either copper or zinc. Iron nails are sometimes used, but they are very liable to rust, and so after a short time become of no use. All slates ought to be fastened with two nails. Doubles and Ladies are sometimes fastened with only one, on account of their smallness, but it is inferior work.

The Welsh slates are generally considered the best, and are of a light sky-blue colour. Westmoreland slates are of a greenish hue. It frequently happens, when roofs are covered with these slates, that the slater has to deal with those of various sizes, and of course this requires more skill, for he not only has to arrange them so that they shall break joint one with another, but the lathing must also be gauged accordingly. In this case the largest and thickest slates are hung at the bottom, and the smallest and thinnest at the top, nearest the ridge; and a great deal of care must be taken in trimming and sorting them.

The gauge is taken in the same way as other kinds of slating, that is, according to the length.

The following is a table of sizes and gauges of roofing slates :—

| Names. | Size. | | Gauge in Inches. | Weight per Square. | Number per Square. | |
	Length.	Breadth.			Slates.	Nails.
	ft. in.	ft. in.		lbs.		
Doubles . .	1 1	0 6	$5\frac{1}{2}$	672	480	960
Ladies . . .	1 4	0 8	7	886	300	600
Countesses .	1 8	0 10	$8\frac{1}{2}$	657	180	360
Duchesses. .	2 0	1 0	$10\frac{1}{2}$	712	130	260
Rags, Queens and West-morelands, of various sizes . .	A square of these weighs about half a ton.					

The methods of hanging slates vary according to the different situations and also the slates that are used. But in all plain work it is best, if possible, to strain a line for the eaves' course, and so fix the slates to it; also, to run each course horizontally throughout the length of the roof. This is done by gauging the margin of the course at each end upon the first course, and straining a chalked line from end to end, so making a mark

E

for a guide to get the second course perfectly straight and parallel with the first.

When the roof is slated as high up as it is possible to reach from the eaves, a scaffold is erected. This is sometimes done with a scaffold-pole, or a piece of quartering being hung from the ridge-tree with scaffold-cords. But it is much better to make it with hanging trestles in the form of an equal-sided triangle, with an iron hook at the top, so as to fasten it to the ridge with cords; after which scaffold-boards are laid upon them. This will be a much more convenient scaffold than the previous one, and is easily raised or lowered as required. For all hips and valleys it is usual to fix the trimming-block to one of the rafters or somewhere convenient, so that each slate can be cut according to the shape required without the necessity of going off the roof.

It is sometimes thought best to point slating inside with lime and hair; but, certainly, if the slating is properly executed, this is unnecessary; and if it is to keep out the little wind that would otherwise pass between them one would think they would be better without it, for we all know how very hot buildings that are slated usually are, particularly in summer time.

PLASTERER.

The business of the plasterer chiefly consists in covering walls, ceilings, brick or wood partitions, floors, &c., with cements, limes, and plaster, in order to bring them to a uniform surface to re-

ceive the painting, paper-hanging, or distemper-
ing.   This part is usually done by the bricklayer
in small towns and villages, but in London it
forms a separate trade.   But the decorative portions of the finishing of buildings, such as running cornices, mouldings, making and fixing
centre flowers, &c., is almost exclusively done by
the plasterer.   All internal plastering, as a rule,
is done with chalk lime, hair, plaster of Paris,
and Keen's and Martin's cements.   The following
are the different methods of mixing them :—

  Lime and Hair, or Coarse Stuff.—For this purpose the sand should be clean, sharp, and screened.
Then form a pan to receive the lime.   This is
slacked in a tub, and sufficient water is afterwards
added to bring it to the consistence of cream, and
is then run through a fine sieve into the pan
formed with the sand.   After a sufficient quantity
is run out to carry the sand, the hair is thrown
into the lime, and thoroughly raked about with a
two-pronged rake, so as to part the hair and mix
it well with the mortar; but it would be better
to run the lime into putty, as for fine stuff, and
when cold mix the hair with it; this will not be
so apt to rot the hair, and so add to the stability
of the work.

For this purpose bullocks' hair is generally
used, and this should be well beaten with small
laths, or else laid in water a day or two before it
is mixed with the lime.   The whole is then
mixed, and allowed to lie for a short time.

Fine Stuff, or Putty, is made of pure lime, and

is mixed in the same way as lime used for coarse stuff; but instead of running it into a pan of sand, this is run into a " putty bin," built with bricks according to the size required, and allowed to remain there until the evaporation of the water has brought it to a proper thickness for use : if the water rise to the top, it can be drawn off if required, and the putty will get dry the sooner.

For lime stucco the sand is mixed with the putty according to the quantity required. This stucco, when left for painting, is left smooth from the trowel. When plaster of Paris is to be used for the purpose of setting either coarse or fine stuff, the mortar or putty is made into a little pan in the banker. The water is poured in, and afterwards the plaster, so that the latter is well soaked before it is mixed with the mortar. This is called gauged stuff, and is used for running cornices, mouldings, and in fact all kinds of work which ought to be finished by one operation.

The various cements and other compositions made use of by the plasterer are very numerous; but those principally used for inside decorations, are Keen's, Martin's, and Parian cements; these are well adapted for plastering where hardness and beautiful finish are required; Keen's cement is used for skirtings, dados, angle beads, &c., because of its extreme hardness.

Portland, Roman, and lias cements are those generally in use for all external plastering; and as regards quality and cheapness, Portland is decidedly the best.

All enrichments, such as flowers or fruit cornices, centre flowers, &c., are first moulded in clay and afterwards cast in plaster of Paris, or made of *papier-mâché*.

The Operations of Plastering.—Almost the first thing the plasterer does is the lathing, so he can get all the woodwork rendered first, as this takes longer to dry than the brickwork. And for this purpose he uses *single*, one and a half, and double laths. These names denote the different thicknesses. The laths are generally of fir. Care ought to be taken that the thickest laths are used for the ceilings, on account of there being a greater strain when in an horizontal position than when upright. The first coat of plastering of coarse stuff upon the laths of ceilings is called *pricking up*, and is used very stiff, to prevent its dropping off again.

But the first coat on walls is the *rendering;* the second the *screeding, or floating,* from its being brought to a level surface with the screeding rule and hand-float; and the third or last is called the *setting* or *fining off.*

The first coat is laid on rough, and afterwards scratched with a piece of lath, to form a key for the second coat. The operation of floating walls is performed by fixing upright stripes of plastering about 6 or 8 inches wide, and about 6 feet apart, if only one man is to work upon them; these form the screeds: and the method of obtaining them is by setting small pieces of plaster at each angle of the wall that is to be plastered. These

are called "dots," and the dot nearest the ceiling
should be plumb with that nearest the floor;
after this a line is drawn along the ceiling from
one to the other, and the intermediate ones fixed
to it. Then repeat the operation with those dots
nearest the floor; these ought to be gauged with
a little plaster of Paris, so as to make them set
quicker; the screeds may then be filled up, and
floated level with these dots. The bays formed by
the screeds may then be plastered with coarse
stuff, and floated perfectly level with the floating
rule. The second coating of ceilings is performed
in the same way, only one is upright and the
other is level.

In two-coat work the rendering and screeding
are performed at one time upon brickwork. After
the work has been brought to a level surface with
the floating-rule, should there be any deficiencies
caused by stones or knots of hair, they are made
good with the hand-float.

Sometimes it is thought best to either sweep
the floated work, or else put a nail through the
float, so as to project a little on the face of it, and
then rub it over the work, and so give it a key
for the fine stuff. The floating should be allowed
to get hard, but not too dry, before the fine stuff
is laid on; at all events, unless the wall is in a
damp situation, it ought to be sprinkled with
water from the stock-brush. Fine stuff is sometimes laid on with the laying-on trowel, and
sometimes with the hand-float, at all events the
latter is used to bring the fine stuff to a regular

surface before it is trowelled off.   This is done by
well rubbing it, either with the laying-on or
gauging trowel, alternately wetting it with the
stock-brush until a fine and smooth surface is
obtained.   Stucco, which is left smooth on the
face, and gauge stuff, are treated in the same way.

All work left from the trowel ought to be watched
for a day or two, and if any small cracks are seen,
they ought to be well wetted and trowelled over;
but these are seldom seen in stucco work, the sand
preventing this to a great extent.

Rough Stucco is sometimes used for halls, stair-
cases, passages, &c.; this is left from the float,
and sometimes a little extra sand is put with the
finishing coat; but in other respects it is
executed in the same way as smooth stucco.

Laid Work.—This is simply a coat of coarse
stuff laid upon brickwork, or lathing, to receive
limewhiting or colouring, and is often done in
cellars, outhouses, &c., where a better kind of
plastering is thought unnecessary.   If cellar
ceilings are covered with this rough plastering.
it prevents the wind from passing through the
floor-boards to the rooms above, which is often
very uncomfortable.   But of late years it has
become the practice to make the floors fireproof
as well as airproof; and this is sometimes done
by "pugging," that is, lining the spaces between
the floor-joist with concrete two or three inches
thick; and to receive this, fillets are nailed on
each side of the joists, and a rough boarding is
laid upon them.

Portland cement is used by the plasterer to a great extent for making floors, and there is little doubt of its answering that purpose if it is laid sufficiently thick, and the materials are gauged in a proper manner. For this purpose (as well as all others) the cement ought to be gauged with sharp sand, *free from clay*, in equal quantities, both for the first coat and also for the second; for if the first coat is gauged with a greater quantity of sand than the second, they will not bind together; besides pure cement swells more in setting than cement and sand does when mixed up together; therefore if the finishing coat is made finer than the first, it will be very liable to blister, and so destroy the floor. The sand for the last coat ought to be well washed, and the two coats need not exceed an inch in thickness. In many parts of England, where there are plaster mills in the vicinity, it is usual to lay floors of that material. But this plaster is of a much rougher kind than that which is generally used; in fact it is a sort of dross from the mills. These floors are laid about 2 inches or $2\frac{1}{2}$ inches in thickness, and finished at one operation. A plaster floor of Welsh lime is thought to be equally as good as grey plaster, and can be done for one-third less.

In some of the eastern counties the fronts of houses are plastered with a rough stucco, and while it is damp well dashed with small stones; this answers very well for renewing old fronts, where they have previously been plastered, for by pulling off the old mortar, and replastering and dashing it, the front will be well repaired and still retain its original appearance.

Plastering may be summed up as follows:— The commonest kind of work consists of only one coat, this is called *rendering* on brickwork, and *laying*, if on laths; when a second coat is added, it becomes two-coat work, as *render set*, or *lath lay and set*; and when the work is floated, it is three-coat work, and is *lath lay float and set* for ceilings and partitions, and *render float and set* for brick-work.

The following remarks may be found useful:—

100 yards of lathing require 20 bundles of laths and 7,600 nails.

100 yards of *rendering*, or *laying*, 20 bushels of chalk lime, 40 bushels of sand, and 3 bushels of hair.

100 yards of *floating* requires about half as much as rendering.

And *setting* requires 10 bushels of lime, 2 bushels of white hair and a little sand if required.

Render set requires per 100 yards, 30 bushels of lime, 42 bushels of sand, and 5 bushels of hair.

Render float and set, 40 bushels of lime, 62 bushels of sand, and 7 bushels of hair, to 100 yards.

A bushel and a half of Portland cement will plaster two yards superficial three-quarters of an inch thick.

ARTIFICIAL STONE.

The following may be found very useful, both on account of its cheapness, simplicity, and durability :—

Take 7 parts of coke dust, screened through a quarter bar screen, to 1 part of Portland cement, for all kinds of ornamental purposes, such as small columns, capitals, balustrades, mouldings for cornices, chimney-pieces, &c. But for pavement, steps, window-sills, hearth-stones, or any rougher kind of work, 5 parts of coke dust, and 3 parts of any hard substance, such as burnt earth, broken brick, &c.; but these also should be screened before they are mixed with the cement. Moulds are then made of wood, or in some cases iron, to the shape required, care being taken that they are a little smaller at the bottom than they are at the top, so that the moulded work shall turn out of the mould freely when set ; the moulds should be well greased first, and a little pure cement mixed up very thin thrown into them ; the cement and coke dust, or cement, coke dust, and broken bricks, are then mixed with water to form a sort of concrete, and gently put into the moulds; if this is done properly the soft, pure cement will flow all round the inside of the mould, and so give a facing to the coarser stuff; the top is finished off level with the mould with the trowel. This work should be left until it is perfectly hard, which will take two or three days. There is one fault attached to this composition, that is, when it is used for

steps, stair-cases, or pavement, it is liable to get
very smooth and slippery; but in other respects it
answers very well.

DISTEMPERING OF CEILINGS, WALLS, ETC.

For this purpose the work should be well washed
with clean water and scraped with the trowel, so
as to thoroughly clean off all old whitening. Of
course, if the walls and ceilings are new they do
not require this. After they are dry they should
be *clear-coled*, that is, sized over with clear size,
taking care in melting the size that it does not
boil, but only heated sufficient to melt it. If glue is
used instead of size, put 1½ pints of water to each
pound of glue. When this is done, the work is
ready to receive the whitewash. To mix this,
break the whitening into a vessel containing sufficient water to cover it, and let it soak well, and
if any water remains on the top, pour it off, and
mix the size with the whitening, which will be
about 4 lbs. to the ball, more or less as required;
and strain a little blue-black or ultramarine blue
into the vessel containing them, and well mix the
whole together. This mixing is usually done the
day before the whitening is required for use;
then the size will get set, and by stirring well
before using it, the whole will work up into a
jelly. Should there be any water stains in the
ceilings, they should be well washed with strong
soft soap and water, and if this fail, paint them
previous to white-washing the ceiling. All work
ought to receive two coats.

SECTION VI.

PRACTICAL GEOMETRY AND MENSURATION.

THE problems here given are those only which it is absolutely necessary for the bricklayer to understand before he can be considered a proficient tradesman.

1. A *solid* is a figure, or a body having three dimensions, viz., length, breadth, and thickness. The boundaries of a solid are surfices or superficies.

2. A *superficies*, or surfice, has length and breadth only; the boundaries of a surfice are lines.

3. A *line* is length without breadth, and is formed by the motion of a point. The extremities of a line are points.

5. A *point* is that which has no parts or magnitude; it is indivisible; it has no length, breadth, nor thickness.

6. When a straight line, B D, standing on
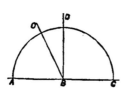
another, A C, makes the angle D B A equal to the angle D B C, each of these angles is called a right angle; the measure of the angle D B A is 90 degrees, or the fourth part of 360 degrees.

7. An *acute angle* is less than a right angle, as D B O.

8. An *obtus. angle* is greater than a right angle, as C B O.

9. A *plane triangle* is the space in-closed by three straight lines, and has three angles, as B.

10. A right-angled triangle is that which has one of its angles right as A B C; the side A C opposite the right angle is called the hypo-thenuse, the side B C the perpen-dicular, and B A the base.

11. An *obtuse-angled triangle* has one of its angles obtuse, as the tri-angle C.

12. An *acute-angled triangle* has all its three angles acute, as shown in figure B.

13. An *equilateral triangle* has all its sides and angles equal as D.

14. An *isosceles triangle* is that which has two of its sides equal, as E.

15. A *scaline triangle* is that which has all its sides unequal, as F.

16. A *square* is a four-sided figure having all its sides equal and all its angles right.

17. An *oblong*, or *rectangle*, is a right angled parallelogram, whose length exceeds its breadth, as G.

18. A *rhombus* is a parallelogram having all its sides equal, but its angles are not right angles, as H.

19. A *rhomboid* is a parallelo-gram having its opposite sides equal, but its angles are not right-angles, and its length exceeds its breadth, as I.

20. A *trapezium* is a figure included by four straight lines, no two of which are parallel to each other, as K. A line connecting any two of its opposite angles is called a diagonal.

21. A *trapezoid* is a four-sided figure having two of its opposite sides parallel, as M.

22. *Polygons* are those which have more than four sides. They receive particular names from the number of their sides; thus a *pentagon* has five sides, a *hexagon* has six sides, a *heptagon* seven, an *octagon* eight, a *nonagon* nine, a *decagon* ten, an *undecagon* eleven, and a *dodecagon* has twelve sides.

If all the sides of each figure are equal, it is called a regular polygon; but if unequal, an irregular polygon.

23. A *circle* is a plane figure contained by one line, called its circumference, which is every-where equally distant from a point within it called its centre, as o; and an *arc* of a circle is any part of its circumference, as A B.

24. The *diameter* of a circle is a straight line

passing through the centre and terminated both
ways by the circumference; thus
A B is the diameter of the circle;
the diameter divides the circle
into two equal parts, each of
which is called a semicircle:
the diameter also divides the
circumference into two equal
parts each containing 180 degrees.

Any line drawn from the centre perpendicular
to A B, it divides the semicircle into two equal
parts, A O s and B O s, each of which is called a
quadrant, or one-fourth of a circle; and the arcs
A s and B s contain each 90 degrees; and they
are said to be the measure of the angles A O s and
B O s.

25. A *chord* of an arc is a straight line joining
its extremities, and is less than the diameter; c B
is the chord of the arc c D B, or of the arc c A s B.

26. A *segment* of a circle is that part of the
circle contained between the chord and the circumference, and may be greater or less than a
semicircle.

Problem I.

*From a given point, P, in a
straight line, A B, to erect a
perpendicular.*

1. On each side of the point,
P, take equal portions, P *x*, P *f*;
and from the centres, x *f*, with any radius greater

than P *x*, describe two arcs, cutting each other at D; then the line joining D P will be perpendicular to A B.

When the point, P, *is at the end of the line.*

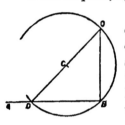

2. From any centre, c, out of the line, and with the distance, c B, as radius, describe a circle, cutting A B in D, draw D C O, and the line joining the points O B will be perpendicular to A B.

Or thus:

Set one leg of the compasses on B, and with any extent, B P, describe an arc, P *x*; set off the same extent from P to *q*; join P *q*; from *q* as centre with the extent, P *q*, as radius describe an arc *r*, and the line joining *r* B will be perpendicular to A B.

PROBLEM II.

Upon a given right line to describe an equilateral triangle.

Let A B be the given right line. From the centres A and B, with the given line A B as radius, describe two arcs cutting each other at c; then the line drawn from the point c to the points

A and B will form with the line A B the triangle required.

PROBLEM III.

To describe a triangle, having the length of the three sides given.

Let A B, C D, E F, be the given lines, of which A B is the base line. From B as centre with C D as radius describe an arc, and from A as centre with E F as radius describe another arc, cutting the first at G; join A G, G B: this will give the triangle required.

PROBLEM IV.

To find the centre of a given circle.

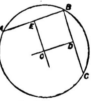

Draw any two chords A B, B C, and divide each into two equal parts, as shown at E and D; draw the lines E O and O D at right angles to A B and B C, and where these lines intersect at O will be the centre of the given circle A B C.

PROBLEM V.

To describe a regular pentagon upon a given line.

Let A B be the given line. With B as centre and B A as radius describe the semicircle A C D; then with A as centre, with same radius, describe an arc cutting the semicircle in C; bisect A B at E, join C E, bisect the arc C B in F, join E F; then

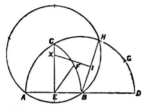

with D as centre, E F for radius, cut the semicircle in G, and with G as centre, with same radius, cut the semicircle in H; draw the line H B and bisect it at I, and at this point erect a perpendicular cutting the line E C in X; this will be the centre of the circumscribing circle.

PROBLEM VI.

To describe a regular hexagon upon a given line.

Let A B be the given line. With·A as centre

and A B as radius describe an arc, and with B as centre with same radius describe a second arc, cutting the first in C; this point of intersection is the centre of the circumscribing circle.

TABLE OF POLYGONS.

No. of Sides.	Name of Polygon.	Multiplier or Divisor.
5	Pentagon	1—7 decimals
6	Hexagon	2—0 or radius
7	Heptagon.	2—3
8	Octagon	2—62
9	Nonagon	2—9
10	Decagon	3—247
11	Undecagon	3—55
12	Dodecagon	3—84

The preceding Table may be found useful in describing regular polygons of any number of sides, from five to twelve inclusive.

Description of the above Table.

In the left-hand column will be found the number of sides of any polygon having from five to twelve sides. In the second column will be found the name of the polygon corresponding with the number in the first column. And the third column contains those figures by which the length of the side must be multiplied for the diameter of the circumscribing circle ; or by which the length of the diameter of a given circle must be divided to give the length of the side of each polygon in a line with it in the opposite column.

Examples.

What is the length of each side of a regular pentagon, the diameter of the circumscribing circle being 4 feet ?

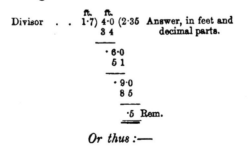

Or thus :—

What is the diameter of the circumscribing

circle of a nonagon, each side being 2 feet in
length ?

2 feet length of side.
2·9 multiplier.
————
1 8

4
————
5·8 Answer.

Therefore the diameter of the circle is 5 feet
and 8-10ths of a foot, which is equal to 5 feet
9 inches and 5-8ths of an inch.

Problem VII.

*To describe an ellipsis, having the longest diameter
given.*

Let A B be the given diameter.   Erect the perpendicular C D, and divide A B into four equal

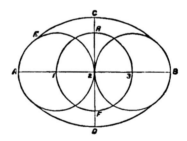

parts at 1, 2, 3; then with 1 2 3 as centres, with
radius 1 2, describe the three circles as shown;
then from F as centre with F E as radius describe
the arc c, and with H as centre with same radius

describe the arc D. This will complete the ellipsis.

Another method of describing an ellipse.

Let A B, C D, be the given diameters drawn at right angles with each other. Then with C as

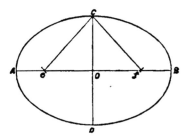

centre with A O as radius describe an arc cutting A B at *e* and *f*; then take a piece of string or very fine wire the length of A B, fix one end at *e* and the other at *f*; then draw the ellipse by running the pencil along the string, taking care the string is kept tight with the pencil.

PROBLEM VIII.

To describe a circle about any triangle.

Bisect any two sides as shown at A and B, and draw perpendicular lines intersecting at C. This point of intersection is the centre from which the circle is drawn.

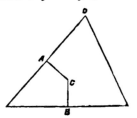

Problem IX.

To inscribe a circle within a triangle.

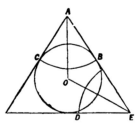

From A as centre with any radius describe an arc B C; bisect it, and through the point of bisection draw the line A o; bisect the angle D E B, and draw the line o E. Where the lines A o and o B intersect is the centre of the circl

Problem X.

In a given circle to inscribe a square.

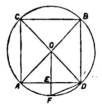

Draw any two diameters, A B, C D, at right angles to each other, then join their extremities, and the figure thus formed will be a square inscribed in a given circle. And if a line be drawn from the centre o, bisecting A D, and produced to F, F D will be the length of one side of an octagon inscribed in the circle.

Problem XI.

In a given circle, to inscribe any regular polygon; or, to divide the circumference of a given circle into any number of equal parts.

Divide the diameter A B into as many equal parts as the figure has sides; erect the perpen-

dicular o s from the centre o; divide the radius o f into four equal parts,
and set off three of these
parts from f to s; draw a
line from s to the second
division h of the diameter
A B, and produce it to cut
the circumference at c; join
A C, and it will be the side
of the polygon required.

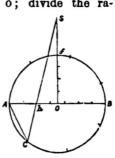

PROBLEM XII.

*To draw a straight line equal to any given arc of a
circle.*

Let A c B be the given arc of
a circle; divide the chord A B
into four equal parts, and set
off one of these parts from B to c; join D c, and it
will be the length of half the given arc, sufficiently near enough for practice.

PROBLEM XIII.

To make a square equal in area to a given circle.

Divide the diameter A B into
fourteen equal parts, and set off
eleven of them from A to c;
from c erect the perpendicular
c D and join A D, the square of
which will be very nearly equal
to the area of the given circle
of which A D B is the half.

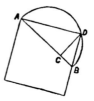

The foregoing geometrical problems are those generally used by the bricklayer; but for those who are anxious to proceed farther, there are many excellent manuals of instruction.

A FEW REMARKS ON MENSURATION OF BRICKLAYERS' WORK.

The area of any plane figure is the space contained within its boundaries, and is estimated by the number of square miles, yards, feet, inches, and parts which it contains. This squaring is generally estimated by the following rules of arithmetic, viz. : duodecimals, or cross multiplication, decimals, and practice.

DUODECIMALS.

Rule 1. Write the multiplier under the multiplicand in such a manner that feet shall be under feet, inches under inches, and parts under parts.

2. Multiply each term of the multiplicand (beginning at the lowest) by the number of feet in the multiplier, and write each result under its respective term, taking care to carry one for every 12 from each lower denomination to its next superior, and set down the remainder under the term last multiplied.

3. Next multiply the terms of the multiplicand by the number under the denomination of inches in the multiplier ; carry 1 for every 12, as before. But set down each remainder one place further to the right than as if multiplied by a number under the denomination of feet.

4. Proceed in the same manner with the second in the multiplier, setting each result one more place further to the right hand, and so on with thirds, fourths, &c.

5. Add the partial products thus obtained up, and their sum will be the product.

Examples.

1. Multiply 4 feet 7 inches by 3 feet 10 inches

	ft.	in.		
	4	7		
	3	10		
	13	9		
	3	9 · 10		
	17	6 · 10		

2. Multiply 37 feet 9 inches 3 parts by 7 feet 6 inches and 5 parts.

	ft.	in.	pts.		
	37	9	3		
	7	6	5		
	264	4	9		
	18	10	7 · 6		
	1	3	8 · 10 · 3		
	284	7	1 · 4 · 3		

	ft.	in.		ft.	in.		ft.	in.	pts.		
3. Multiply	7	6	×	5	9	Answer	43	1	6		
4. Multiply	9	8	×	7	6	,,	72	6			
5. Multiply	7	5 · 9	×	3	5 · 3	,,	25	8	6 · 2 · 3		
6. Multiply	57	9	×	9	5	.,	543	9	9		
7. Multiply	75	9	×	17	7	,,	1331	9	3		

DECIMAL FRACTIONS.

In decimal fractions the integer or whole thing, as one yard, one foot, &c., is supposed to be divided into ten equal parts, and these parts into tenths, and so on without end.

F

These parts are distinguished from the whole
numbers by a point prefixed: thus—·5, which
stands for 5-10ths, or half a whole number; ·25,
which stands for 25-100ths, or one-quarter of a
whole number; or ·75, which stands for 75-100ths,
or three-quarters of a whole number.

Whole numbers increase in ten-fold proportion
to the left hand; decimal parts decrease in ten-
fold proportion to the right hand; so that ciphers
placed before decimal parts decrease their value
by removing them further from the point; or
units placed thus—·5, is 5-10ths; ·05, is 5-100ths;
and ·005, is 5-1000ths. But ciphers after
decimal parts do not alter their value; for ·5, ·50,
·500 are each but 5-10ths, or half a whole
number.

Rule.—In addition of decimals great care must
be taken in setting down the figures to be added
up, so that each figure shall come under another
of the same value, whether this be a mixed
number or pure decimal parts. And, in order to
do this, there must be a due regard had to the
separating points, which ought always to stand
in a direct line one with another; and, to the
right hand of these, carefully place the decimal
parts according to their respective values, and
add them as in whole numbers.

Examples.

To add 5 ft. 9 in., 7 ft. 6 in., 3 ft. 3 in., and
7 ft. 10 in. together.

Ft. Decimal parts.			
5·75	Equal	5 ft.	9 in.
7·5	,,	7 ft.	6 in.
3·25	,.	3 ft.	3 in.
7·835	,,	7 ft.	10 in.

24·335 Answer, equal 24 ft. 4 in.

SUBTRACTION OF DECIMALS.

This differs but very little from whole numbers, only in placing the numbers, which must be carefully observed, as in addition.

Examples.

Subtract 2·395 from 7·62, and 5 ft. 9 in. from 27 ft. 3 in.

7·620		27·25
2·395		5·75

5·225 Answer.   21·50 = 21 ft. 6 in.

1. From	·769 take	·543	Answer	·226
2. From	1·743 take	·339	Answer	1·404
3. From	3·975 take	1·243	Answer	2·732
4. From	407·2 take	49·362	Answer	357·838

MULTIPLICATION OF DECIMALS.

Rule.—Place the decimal parts, and multiply them as in whole numbers; and from the product cut off as many figures towards the right hand as there are figures representing decimal parts, both in the multiplier and multiplicand together; but should there not be so many places in the product,

make up the defect by adding ciphers towards the
left hand.

Examples.

Multiply   3·795   Multiply 5 ft. 6 in. × 8 ft. 10 in.
By   2·43   5·5
                            8·835
          ‾‾‾‾‾‾   ‾‾‾‾‾‾
          11385
          15180   275
          7590   165
          ‾‾‾‾‾‾   440
          9·22185   440
                        ‾‾‾‾‾‾‾‾‾‾‾‾‾‾‾‾‾‾‾‾‾‾‾
                        48·5925 . = 48 ft. 7¼ in.
                        ‾‾‾‾‾‾‾‾‾‾‾‾‾‾‾‾‾‾‾‾‾‾‾

Multiply   3·074 × 25·93   Answer   79·70882
Multiply   25·15 × 72·04   Answer 1811·8060
Multiply   ·07 × 1·02   Answer   ·0714

DIVISION OF DECIMALS.

This is worked in the same way as whole
numbers, the only difficulty is in valuing the
quotient.

Rule 1.—The first figure in the quotient is
always of the same value with that figure of the
dividend which answers or stands over the place
of units in the divisor.

Rule 2.—The quotient should always have as
many decimals as the dividend has more than the
divisor.

Note 1.—If the divisor and dividend have both
the same number of decimal parts, the quotient
will be a whole number.

Note 2.—If the dividend has not so many
places of decimals as there are in the divisor,

then so many ciphers must be added to the
dividend as will make them equal, and the quotient will then be a whole number.

Note 3.—And if, when the sum is done, the
quòtient has not so many figures as it should have
places of decimals, then so many ciphers must be
added as there are places wanting.

Brickwork is estimated at the rate of a brick
and a half thick; this is called the standard thickness, so that if a wall is either more or less than
this thickness it must be reduced to it; thus:—
Multiply the superficial contents of the wall by
the number of half-bricks in thickness, and
divide the product by 3.

When a piece of brickwork is to be measured,
the first thing to be done is to ascertain what
measures are to be employed: then, having multiplied the length and breadth together, if the
dimensions are feet, the product is divided by the
divisor agreed upon, this is generally 272¼ feet
to the rod standard thickness, and the quotient
will be the number of rods and feet contained
within the dimensions taken.

In measuring work by the rod of 272¼ feet, it
is very seldom the odd quarter is used, owing to
its taking more labour in figuring for a mere
trifle.

Examples.

How many rods of brickwork (standard thickness) are there in a wall 34 feet 6 inches long by
23 feet 9 inches high, at 1½ bricks thick?

DUODECIMALS.

```
ft.  in.
34   6
23   9
─────────
102  0
68   0
11   6
25  10 · 6
```

272) 819   4 · 6 (3 rds. 3 ft. 4½ in. Answer.
      816
     ─────────
       3

DECIMALS.

```
ft.
34 · 5
23 · 75
─────────
1725
2415
1035
690
```

272) 819 · 375 (3 · 0124* rds. Answer.
      816
     ─────────
       337
       272
     ─────────
       655
       544
     ─────────
       1110
       1088
     ─────────
        · 22
```

If the area of a wall be 3,700 feet, and the thickness 2½ bricks, how many rods and feet does it contain ?

* This decimal fraction equals 3 ft. 4½ in.
```

Example.

```
          3700 feet the area, by
             5 half-bricks thick.
                ─────────
Standard divisor 3) 18500
                ─────────
          272) 6166 (22 rds.
                544
               ─────
                726
                544   .
               ─────
                182 feet.
```

CHIMNEY SHAFTS.

In measuring *chimney breasts*, when standing against any party wall, it is usual to take the width of the middle for the breadth, and the height of the story for the length: the thickness should be the same as the depth of the jambs; and if the chimney is carried up square to the ceiling no deductions are made for the fire-place on account of the extra labour in gathering the with walls over to prepare for the hearth in the room above.

The chimney-shaft, or that portion which is above the roof, is measured by multiplying the height, width, and depth together. But in cases where there is a greater amount of labour than usual, the quality of the work is taken into consideration, and the price allowed according to its class.

Chimney Shafts in the Form of a Circle.—In order to measure these it is necessary to obtain the diameter of the shaft midway between the base and the top as they are usually battering. Square this diameter, and multiply the product by the decimal ·7854*; this will give the area of the circle, after cutting off the four fingers from the right hand; and this area multiplied by the height will give the contents in cubic feet.

Example.

What is the cubic contents of a shaft the mean diameter of which is 4 feet and the height 60 feet?

```
        4      diameter.
        4
       16      square of diameter.
    ·7854      decimal fraction.
      ____
       64
       80
      128
      112
    _____
   12·5664     area of circle.
      60       height.
   _____
  753·9840     cubic contents.
```

The diameter of a circle is to its circumference as 7 is to 22; therefore, if the diameter is not to be obtained by any other means, take the girth or circumference of the shaft, and as 22 is to 7, so is the circumference to the diameter.

Example.

Let the girth of a circular shaft be 10 feet, then, by proportion, the diameter will be obtained in the following manner :—

* This decimal fraction equals the area of any circle whose diameter is 1, *i.e.* if the diameter of the circle is 1 foot, this fraction of a foot is the area.

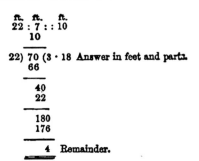

```
  ft.  ft.   ft.
  22 : 7 : : 10
         10
       ─────
22) 70 (3 · 18 Answer in feet and parts.
    66
    ─────
      40
      22
     ─────
      180
      176
     ─────
        4  Remainder.
```

When the shaft is in the form of a regular polygon, the following table may be found useful for the purpose of ascertaining its area in feet or inches :—

Rule.—Square the length of the side of the polygon, and multiply the product by those figures in a line with the figure in the first column denoting the number of sides of the given polygon ; the product thus obtained will be the area. And this multiplied by the height of the chimney will give the cubic contents. And to bring this into rods, divide by 306 feet.

Number of Sides.	Multiplier.
3	·433
5	1·72
6	2·698
7	3·634
8	4·828
9	6·182
10	7·694
11	9·366
12	11·196

Vaulting.—In measuring circular, elliptical, or Gothic vaulting, the rule is to find the superficial contents of one end, and multiply it by the length of the vault; or, take a piece of string or the tape, and ply it close to the soffit from one side of the vault to the other, and this length by the length of the vault will give the superficial contents of soffit; then multiply by the thickness for standard or cubic contents. But if this method is employed, the outside surface *ought* to be taken as well as the soffit. Add the two areas together, and divide by 2 for the exact superficial contents, and then multiply by the thickness for standard or cubic contents, as before explained.

Groins are generally measured by taking the length and breadth of the base and multiplying them together, and that product by the height. But sometimes one-tenth is deducted from the solidity thus found, and the remainder is reckoned as the solid contents.

But if measuring for labour only, the groin-points are measured by running measures, the price being so much per foot.

Bakers' Ovens.—It is usual in measuring these to cube the whole and divide by 306 to bring it to rods.

A TABLE OF BRICKWORK,

Showing how many rods, feet, and inches are contained in any number of superficial feet, from 1 foot to 10,000 feet, and so on as far as required;

and from half a brick to two bricks, and, by addition, to any thickness.

This table also shows how many bricks are required to build a piece of brickwork, from 1 foot to 10,000 feet, from half a brick to two bricks, and this also, by addition only, to any thickness or number of feet required, at the rate of 16·544 bricks to the foot standard thickness, or 4500 to the rod.

Explanation of the following Table.

At the head of this table, over each separate column, is stated the thickness of any wall from half a brick to two bricks, and beneath each of these is a double column, one for giving the rods, feet, and inches, contained in the wall, and the other the number of bricks contained in these rods, feet, and inches, standard measurement; and in the first column towards the left hand will be found the number of feet the wall contains by superficial measurement.

TABLE OF BRICKWORK.

Feet super-ficial	Half Brick Thick.				One Brick Thick.				One and a Half Brick Thick.				Two Bricks Thick.			
	Rds.	ft.	in.	Number of Bricks.	Rds.	ft.	in.	Number of Bricks.	Rds.	ft.	in.	Number of Bricks.	Rds.	ft.	in.	Number of Bricks.
1	0	0	4	6	0	0	8	11	0	1	0	16	0	1	4	22
2	0	0	8	11	0	1	4	22	0	2	0	33	0	2	8	44
3	0	1	0	16	0	2	0	33	0	3	0	49	0	4	0	66
4	0	1	4	22	0	2	8	44	0	4	0	66	0	5	4	88
5	0	1	8	27	0	3	4	55	0	5	0	82	0	6	8	110
6	0	2	0	33	0	4	0	66	0	6	0	99	0	8	0	132
7	0	2	4	38	0	4	8	77	0	7	0	116	0	9	4	154
8	0	2	8	44	0	5	4	88	0	8	0	132	0	10	8	176
9	0	3	0	49	0	6	0	99	0	9	0	149	0	12	0	198
10	0	3	4	55	0	6	8	110	0	10	0	165	0	13	4	220
11	0	3	8	61	0	7	4	121	0	11	0	181	0	14	8	241
12	0	4	0	66	0	8	0	132	0	12	0	198	0	16	0	264
13	0	4	4	72	0	8	8	143	0	13	0	215	0	17	4	286
14	0	4	8	77	0	9	4	154	0	14	0	231	0	18	8	308
15	0	5	0	82	0	10	0	165	0	15	0	248	0	20	0	330
16	0	5	4	88	0	10	8	176	0	16	0	264	0	21	4	352
17	0	5	8	93	0	11	4	187	0	17	0	281	0	22	8	374
18	0	6	0	99	0	12	0	198	0	18	0	297	0	24	0	396
19	0	6	4	104	0	12	8	209	0	19	0	314	0	25	4	418

TABLE—*continued.*

Feet super-ficial	Half Brick Thick.				One Brick Thick.				One and a Half Brick Thick.				Two Bricks Thick.			
	Rds.	ft.	in.	Number of Bricks.	Rds.	ft.	in.	Number of Bricks.	Rds.	ft.	in.	Number of Bricks.	Rds.	ft.	in.	Number of Bricks.
20	0	6	8	110	0	13	4	220	0	20	0	330	0	26	8	440
21	0	7	0	116	0	14	0	231	0	21	0	347	0	28	0	462
22	0	7	4	121	0	14	8	242	0	22	0	364	0	29	4	484
23	0	7	8	127	0	15	4	253	0	23	0	380	0	30	8	506
24	0	8	0	132	0	16	0	264	0	24	0	397	0	32	0	528
25	0	8	4	137	0	16	8	275	0	25	0	413	0	33	4	550
26	0	8	8	143	0	17	4	286	0	26	0	430	0	34	8	572
27	0	9	0	148	0	18	0	297	0	27	0	446	0	36	0	594
28	0	9	4	154	0	18	8	308	0	28	0	463	0	37	4	616
29	0	9	8	159	0	19	4	319	0	29	0	479	0	38	8	638
30	0	10	0	165	0	20	0	331	0	30	0	496	0	40	0	661
31	0	10	4	171	0	20	8	341	0	31	0	512	0	41	4	683
32	0	10	8	176	0	21	4	352	0	32	0	529	0	42	8	705
33	0	11	0	182	0	22	0	363	0	33	0	545	0	44	0	726
34	0	11	4	187	0	22	8	374	0	34	0	562	0	45	4	748
35	0	11	8	193	0	23	4	385	0	35	0	579	0	46	8	772
36	0	12	0	198	0	24	0	396	0	36	0	595	0	48	0	794
37	0	12	4	204	0	24	8	408	0	37	0	612	0	49	4	816
38	0	12	8	209	0	25	4	419	0	38	0	628	0	50	8	837

G

TABLE OF BRICKWORK.

Feet super-ficial.	Half Brick Thick.				One Brick Thick.				One and a Half Brick Thick.				Two Bricks Thick.			
	Rds.	ft.	in.	Number of Bricks.	Rds.	ft.	in.	Number of Bricks.	Rds.	ft.	in.	Number of Bricks.	Rds.	ft.	in.	Number of Bricks.
39	0	13	0	215	0	26	0	430	0	39	0	645	0	52	0	860
40	0	13	4	220	0	26	8	440	0	40	0	661	0	53	4	880
41	0	13	8	226	0	27	4	452	0	41	0	678	0	54	8	904
42	0	14	0	231	0	28	0	462	0	42	0	694	0	56	0	925
43	0	14	4	237	0	28	8	474	0	43	0	711	0	57	4	948
44	0	14	8	242	0	29	4	485	0	44	0	727	0	58	8	970
45	0	15	0	248	0	30	0	496	0	45	0	744	0	60	0	993
46	0	15	4	253	0	30	8	507	0	46	0	761	0	61	4	1014
47	0	15	8	259	0	31	4	518	0	47	0	777	0	62	8	1036
48	0	16	0	264	0	32	0	529	0	48	0	794	0	64	0	1068
49	0	16	4	270	0	32	8	540	0	49	0	810	0	65	4	1080
50	0	16	8	275	0	33	4	551	0	50	0	827	0	66	8	1102
51	0	17	0	281	0	34	0	562	0	51	0	843	0	68	0	1124
60	0	20	0	331	0	40	0	661	0	60	0	992	0	80	0	1322
70	0	23	4	386	0	46	8	772	0	70	0	1158	0	93	4	1644
80	0	26	8	441	0	53	4	882	0	80	0	1323	0	106	8	1764
90	0	30	0	496	0	60	0	992	0	90	0	1488	0	120	0	1985
100	0	33	4	551	0	66	8	1102	0	100	0	1654	0	133	4	2205
200	0	66	8	1102	0	133	4	2205	0	200	0	3308	0	266	8	4410

TABLE—continued.

Feet super ficial.	Half Brick Thick.				One Brick Thick.				One and a Half Brick Thick.				Two Bricks Thick.			
	Rds.	ft.	in.	Number of Bricks.	Rds.	ft.	in.	Number of Bricks.	Rds.	ft.	in.	Number of Bricks.	Rds.	ft.	in.	Number of Bricks.
300	0	100	0	1653	0	200	0	3306	1	28	0	4963	1	128	0	6613
400	0	133	4	2205	0	266	8	4411	1	128	0	6617	1	261	4	8823
500	0	166	8	2757	1	61	4	5514	1	228	0	8272	2	122	8	11028
600	0	200	0	3308	1	128	0	6617	2	56	0	9926	2	256	0	13234
700	0	233	4	3860	1	194	8	7720	2	156	0	11580	3	117	4	15440
800	0	266	8	4411	1	261	4	8823	2	256	0	13235	3	250	8	17646
900	1	28	0	4963	2	56	0	9926	3	84	0	14889	4	112	0	19853
1000	1	61	4	5514	2	122	8	11029	3	184	0	16544	4	245	4	22060
2000	2	122	8	11029	4	245	4	22058	7	96	0	33088	9	218	8	44116
3000	3	184	0	16544	7	96	0	33088	11	8	0	49632	14	192	0	66176
4000	4	245	4	22059	9	218	8	44117	14	192	0	66176	19	165	4	88235
5000	6	34	8	27673	12	69	4	55145	18	104	0	82720	24	138	8	110290
6000	7	96	0	33088	14	192	0	66177	22	16	0	99264	29	112	0	132354
7000	8	157	4	38602	17	42	8	77205	25	200	0	115808	34	85	4	154410
8000	9	218	8	44118	19	165	4	88237	29	112	0	132352	39	68	8	176474
9000	11	8	0	49633	22	16	0	99266	33	21	0	148896	44	32	0	198532
10000	12	69	4	55146	24	138	8	110293	36	208	0	165440	49	5	4	220586

Example 1st.

How many rods and feet of standard work are there in a wall 59 feet in length and 12 feet 6 inches in height, and 1½ bricks thick?

RULE.

```
ft.  in.
59   0   the length.
12   6   the height.
────────
708  0
 29  6
────────
737  6   Area.
```

So by these figures we find the superficial area of the wall to be 737 feet 6 inches. Look in the first column towards the left hand for 700, and opposite that in the sixth column will be found 2 rods 156 feet; look again in the first column for 37 feet, and opposite this, in the sixth column, is 37 feet; add the 6 inches, and the product will be as follows:—

```
rods   ft.   in.
 2    156    0
 0     37    6
───────────────
 2    193    6   Answer.
```

Example 2nd.

How many rods, feet, and inches are there in a wall 95 feet long by 17 feet high, at 2 bricks thick?

$95 \times 15 = 1615$; this is the superficial contents of the wall. Look in the first column for the following numbers—1000 feet, 600 feet, and 15 feet; and opposite these respectively, under the heading "Two bricks thick," will be found the following figures, which added up together will give the standard contents of the wall.

rods	ft.	in.
4	245	4
2	256	0
0	20	0
6	521	4 = 7 rds. 249 ft. 4 in.

The quantity of bricks required to build a wall containing any given number of superficial feet is taken in almost the same way.

Example 3rd.

How many bricks are required to build a wall 80 feet long by 27 feet high, at $1\frac{1}{2}$ bricks thick ?

80 × 27 = 2160 feet, the area. Look in the first column for 2000 feet, 100 feet, and 60 feet, and against these respectively, in the column headed " One and a half bricks thick," will be found the following figures, which, by addition only, give the number of bricks that will build the wall.

```
33088
 1654
  992
-----
35734  Answer.
```

The superficial areas of the walls of a house amount to 2649 feet. Now 1200 feet is 2 bricks thick, 900 feet is $1\frac{1}{2}$ brick thick, and 549 is one brick thick : how many bricks did the builder require to build the house ?

Answer, by table, 47403.

All gauge-work is measured by superficial measurement (unless otherwise specified); and every part that is exposed to view is taken in the dimensions.

Skewbacks, birds'-mouths, splays, beads, &c., are generally measured by the run. But if measured as gauge-work, it is usual to ply the tape, or a piece of string, close to every part of the brick that is moulded, and afterwards measure it to get the whole of the girth of the work, and this is multiplied by the length for the contents.

Arches are also measured by the girth multiplied by the length.

1000 new stock bricks stacked in bolts measure 50 feet cubic.

1000 old bricks cleaned and stacked in bolts measure 72 cubic feet.

SHORT AND USEFUL TABLE.

277¼	cubic inches 1 gallon of water.	
1	cubic foot contains 6 gallons 1¾ pints.	
144	square inches equal 1 square foot.	
1728	cubic inches	,, 1 cubic foot.
9	square feet	,, 1 square yard.
27	cubic feet	,, 1 cubic yard or load.
100	superficial feet	,, 1 square.

Tiling and Slating is measured by the square of 100 feet, and in many country places double measure is allowed for cutting hips and valleys, *i.e.* for *valleys* take the length of the ridge for one dimension and the depth from ridge to eaves for the other, and multiply one by the other for the superficial area; and for *hips* take the length of the eaves and multiply the depth as before. This

PRACTICAL GEOMETRY AND MENSURATION. 115

is so allowed to pay for the amount of waste in labour and material in cutting them.

But in London slating is not measured in this way, but for all hips, valleys, eaves, cuttings to skew gables, cheeks of dormers, &c., the length of the cutting is taken, and 1 foot allowed for the hips and valleys, and 6 inches allowed for eaves and the other cuttings above named. All plain work is measured net.

When the space taken up by sky-lights, chimney-shafts, &c., do not exceed 4 feet in area, no deductions are made on account of the extra labour in cutting round them.

The ridge is always taken separately at per running foot.

Where soakers are used they are reckoned by the dozen.

All plain or pantiling for roofs is measured by the square, and cutting and eaves are allowed for in the same way as slating.

Plain and ornamental tiling for floors, walls, ceilings, &c., is measured by the yard square, and all cutting per foot run.

Plastering is either measured by the foot, yard, or square of 100 feet, and any surface under 1 foot (in taking reveils, &c.) is usually called a foot.

Cornices, beads, chamfers, and all mouldings are taken by the foot run.

Mitres, stop, &c., are taken separately and priced at so much each.

Doorways, windows, fireplaces, &c., are de-

ducted, and ceiling and walls are measured sepa
rately.

Whitewashing and colouring are measured in
the same way as plain plastering—mostly by the
yard square—and where this is done between
principals, rafters, joists, &c., the tape must be
applied to the whole of the surface covered by the
brush.

This work is specified to be one, two, or three
coat work.

THE END.

PRINTED BY J. S. VIRTUE AND CO., LIMITED, CITY ROAD, LONDON.

Printed in the United States
138418LV00010B/40/A

9 781437 047226